用英语讲中国好故事

神话故事（汉英对照）

THE MYTHS STORIES

韩　进　韩　春 ◎ 编著
丁立福　汤　靖 ◎ 译

北京师范大学出版集团
安徽大学出版社

图书在版编目（CIP）数据

神话故事：汉英对照／韩进，韩春编著；丁立福，汤靖译．—合肥：安徽大学出版社，2022.2
（用英语讲中国好故事）
ISBN 978-7-5664-2383-2

Ⅰ．①神… Ⅱ．①韩… ②韩… ③丁… ④汤… Ⅲ．①神话—作品集—中国—汉、英 Ⅳ．① I277.5

中国版本图书馆 CIP 数据核字（2022）第 032808 号

神话故事：汉英对照 韩 进 韩 春 编著
SHENHUA GUSHI: HANYING DUIZHAO 丁立福 汤 靖 译

出版发行：	北京师范大学出版集团
	安 徽 大 学 出 版 社
	（安徽省合肥市肥西路 3 号 邮编 230039）
	www.bnupg.com.cn
	www.ahupress.com.cn
印　　刷：	安徽昶颉包装印务有限责任公司
经　　销：	全国新华书店
开　　本：	170mm×240mm
印　　张：	14.5
字　　数：	230 千字
版　　次：	2022 年 2 月第 1 版
印　　次：	2022 年 2 月第 1 次印刷
定　　价：	41.90 元

ISBN 978-7-5664-2383-2

策划编辑：李 梅 韦 玮 葛灵知　　装帧设计：丁 健
责任编辑：葛灵知 韦 玮　　　　　美术编辑：李 军
责任校对：高婷婷　　　　　　　　　责任印制：赵明炎

版权所有　侵权必究
反盗版、侵权举报电话：0551-65106311
外埠邮购电话：0551-65107716
本书如有印装质量问题，请与印制管理部联系调换。
印制管理部电话：0551-65106311

前　言

青少年是在故事中成长的，听故事、读故事、讲故事，是他们的最爱。自古流传下来的故事浩如烟海，给青少年挑选故事一定要慎之又慎，必须有益于身心健康，能够帮助他们扣好人生精神成长的第一粒扣子。

中华文化源远流长，在先贤留下的无数文化瑰宝中，神话、寓言、成语、童话和民间故事成为青少年必备的精神食粮，哺育他们成长，在薪火相传中延续中华文化的命脉。

每个民族都有自己的神话、寓言、成语、童话和民间故事，共同构成人类文化的宝库。中国的神话、寓言、成语、童话和民间故事蕴含着的中华文化，历来是世界了解中国的一扇窗户、一面镜子和一条捷径。

为弘扬中华文化，让更多海内外青少年更好地了解中华文化，我们编写了这套"用英语讲中国好故事"丛书。本丛书参照教育部统编语文教材推荐阅读书目的范围和要求，选取经过时间检验的神话、寓言、成语、童话和民间故事等经典篇目进行改编创作，在原汁原味讲述故事的同时，力求情节完整，语言流畅，读起来饶有趣味，又开卷有益。

在编排体例上，兼顾中外读者查询方便，以故事发生的时间顺序排列目录，中英文对照阅读，以清新活泼的风格亲近读者，满足其阅读期待。具体篇目从故事、阅读小贴士和难点词汇三部分进行解析，做到知识性、趣味性、教育性、可读性并重。在篇目选择和改编过程中，作者参阅了有关资料，注意汲取同类选本的编写经验，再根据本丛书读者的定位，进行有针对性地阅读辅导。故事虽然还是那些故事，但与现实的联系更加紧密了。

本丛书致力于让青少年读中华文化故事，推动中华文化"走出去"，构建人类精神家园。本丛书难免会有不足之处，欢迎读者批评指正，以期再版重印时加以修订完善。

韩　进

安徽省文艺评论家协会主席

2022 年 2 月 20 日

目 录
Contents

盘瓠的传说 1

Legend of Pan Hu 3

盘古开天辟地 6

Pan Gu Creating the Heaven and the Earth 7

盘古化生万物 9

Pan Gu Giving Birth to All 10

女娲创造人类 12

Nüwa Creating Human Beings 13

颛顼与共工争帝 15

Zhuanxü and Gonggong Competing for the Throne 16

女娲补天 18

Nüwa Patching the Sky 19

天女散花 21

Heavenly Maidens Scattering Flowers 23

伏羲画卦 26

Fuxi Inventing the Eight Trigrams 28

伏羲降龙 31

Fuxi Subduing the Dragon 32

伏羲结网捕鱼 34

Fuxi Fishing with a Net 35

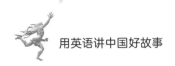

火的"诞生"	37
The Discovery of Fire	39
钻木取火	41
Drilling Woods for Fire	43
击石取火	46
Striking Stones for Fire	48
炎帝教民播百谷	51
Emperor Yan Teaching People to Sow	52
神农尝百草	54
Shennong Tasting Hundreds of Herbs	56
神女瑶姬	59
The Goddess Yaoji	60
太阳神之女	62
Daughter of the Sun God	63
精卫填海	65
Jingwei Filling up the Sea	66
中央之神	68
God of the Central	69
炎黄之战	71
The Battle Between Legendary Emperors	72
蚩尤起兵复仇	74
Chiyou Starting a Revolt	75
黄帝备战蚩尤	77
Yellow Emperor Preparing to Fight Chiyou	78
黄帝大战蚩尤	80
Yellow Emperor Fighting Chiyou	81

刑天舞干戚	83
Xingtian Brandishing His Shield and Battle-ax	84
百鸟朝凤	86
All Birds Paying Homage to the Phoenix	87
百鸟国之王少昊	89
Shaohao, King of Birds	91
管理家仓颉	94
Cangjie Specializing in Management	96
仓颉造字	99
Cangjie Inventing Chinese Characters	101
夸父追日	104
Kuafu Chasing the Sun	105
帝尧出生	107
Birth of Emperor Yao	108
帝尧知人善任	110
Emperor Yao Making Good Use of Able Persons	111
帝尧禅让	113
Emperor Yao Ceding the Throne	114
帝尧嫁女	117
Emperor Yao Marrying His Daughters	119
羿射九日	122
Yi Shooting the Suns	124
羿除六害	127
Yi Eliminating Six Monsters	129
嫦娥奔月	132
Chang'e Flying to the Moon	133

逢蒙杀羿	135
Yi Murdered by Feng Meng	137
河伯与宓妃	140
Hebo and Fufei	141
洛水女神	143
Goddess of Luo River	144
吴刚伐树	146
Wu Gang Cutting the Laurel	148
舜离家出走	151
Shun Escaping from Home	152
舜德行天下	154
Shun's Virtue to the World	155
舜孝行天下	157
Shun's Filial Piety to the World	158
舜变金龙	160
Shun Turning into Golden Dragon	161
舜传位给禹	163
Shun Abdicating the Throne to Yu	164
湘妃竹的传说	166
Legend of Mottled Bamboo	167
鲧偷土治水	169
Gun Controlling Floods by Stealing Xirang	170
鲧治水失败	172
Gun Failing to Control Floods	173
禹子承父业	175
Yu Inheriting His Father's Work	176

禹丈量九州	178
Yu Measuring His Country	180
"河图"和"玉简"的故事	183
Stories of River Map and Jade Tablet	185
禹的婚事	188
Marriage of Yu	189
三过其门而不入	191
Yu Passing by His House Three Times Without Entering	192
启母石的传说	194
Legend of Stone Memorializing Qi's Mother	195
三门峡的由来	197
Origin of Sanmen Xia	198
禹治淮河	200
Yu Harnessing Huai River	201
禹铸九鼎	203
Yu Casting Nine Tripods	204
哪吒闹海	207
Nezha Conquering the Sea	208
宝莲灯传奇	211
Legend of Lotus Lantern	213
沉香救母	216
Chenxiang Saving His Mother	218

盘瓠的传说

中华上古神话中的盘古原型传说不是人，而是一条神犬。

据说在高辛王时代，王后突然得了耳痛病，医治了三年，最终从耳中挑出一只金蚕茧。王后觉得奇怪，就用葫芦瓢盛着，并用盘子盖上，喂养起来。谁想那金蚕茧竟然很快长成了一条五彩斑斓、身长二丈的大狗。高辛王非常喜爱，给它起名"盘瓠"（瓠就是葫芦）。

时逢房王作乱，高辛王就和群臣商量，许诺谁能打败房王，就把公主许配给他。盘瓠听到这话，竟然在夜里潜出宫廷，跑去房王军中，趁房王不备，将其咬死。高辛王大喜过望，准备了很多肉食奖赏盘瓠，但盘瓠一连三天不吃不喝。高辛王问它："莫非你想要我兑现承诺？不是我食言，实在是人犬不能结婚呀！"

想不到，盘瓠突然开口说话："您不用担心，只要把我放在金钟里面七天七夜，我就能变成人，这样就可以娶公主了。"高辛王听了这话，非常诧异，就照盘瓠说的话做了，看它如何变化成人。

一天、两天、三天过去了，到了第六天，公主怕它饿死，悄悄掀开了金钟。只见盘瓠身体已经变成了人，但是脑袋还没有来得及变化，保留着神犬的头。

高辛王遵照前约，让盘瓠和公主结婚。婚后，二人前往人迹罕至的深山岩洞里，隐居下来。公主换上百姓的衣服，亲自做家务，盘瓠每天出去打猎，他们生下三男一女，过着和睦幸福的生活。

由于几个儿女都没有姓氏，于是盘瓠和妻子就请高辛王赐姓。大儿子出生时是用盘子装的，就赐姓"盘"；二儿子出生时是用篮子装的，就赐姓"蓝"；只有三儿子，高辛王想不出合适的姓，正好天上雷声隆隆，于是就赐姓"雷"。

小女儿长大成人,嫁给一个勇敢的士兵,就跟着丈夫姓钟。此后盘、蓝、雷、钟四姓的子孙,繁衍成一个庞大的民族,大家都奉盘瓠为他们共同的老祖宗和保护神。

【阅读小贴士】这个故事的各种版本大同小异,在中国南方瑶、苗、黎等少数民族中流传,人们尊盘瓠为"盘王"。"盘瓠"这两个字的音渐渐转为"盘古"。这个关于盘古来历的幻想神话,填补了盘古开天辟地之前鸿蒙时代的空白,喻示盘古是华夏民族共同的老祖宗。

Legend of Pan Hu

The prototype of Pan Gu in ancient Chinese mythology was said to be a **supernatural** dog instead of a man.

It was said that during the time of King Gao Xin, the queen suddenly got an **excruciating** earache and after three years of medical treatment, a golden cocoon-like thing was finally picked out of her ear. The queen thought it was strange, so she used a **gourd ladle** to hold it, covered it with a plate, and fed it. After a few days, a **mottled**, two-*zhang*-long dog hatched from the cocoon. The king liked the dog so much and named it "Pan Hu" ("Hu" actually is "gourd" in English).

When King Fang was in **rebellion**, King Gao Xin discussed with his ministers and promised to marry the princess to whoever could defeat him. When Pan Hu heard the promise, he surprisingly sneaked out of the palace at night, ran to the army of King Fang and bit him to death by surprise. King Gao Xin was overjoyed and prepared a lot of meat to reward Pan Hu, but the dog refused to eat or drink. For three days, Pan Hu ate nothing. The king asked him, "Do you want me to keep my promise? I'm not breaking my promise, but dogs and humans can't get married!"

supernatural

adj. 神奇的；超自然的

excruciating

adj. 极痛苦的

gourd ladle

(葫芦) 瓢

mottled

adj. 五彩的；斑驳的

rebellion

n. 谋反；叛逆

To the king's surprise, Pan Hu suddenly said, "Don't worry. Just leave me inside the golden bell for seven days and seven nights, and then I will turn into a man and be able to marry the princess." When the king heard this, he was so amazed that he did as Pan Hu asked, and watched how the dog would change into a man.

One day, two days, three days passed, and on the sixth day, fearing that it would die of hunger, the princess quietly lifted the golden bell. The magic was broken when the princess lifted and Pan Hu could not completely turn into a man, while he had a man's body, still possessed a dog's head.

The king followed his previous promise that he allowed the marriage of Pan Hu and the princess. After the marriage, they settled down in the deep mountains, where they lived in **seclusion**. The princess put on the clothes of the common people and did the housework by herself. Her husband went out hunting every day. They had three boys and one girl, and lived a **harmonious** and happy life.

Their sons and daughter had no family names, so Pan Hu and his wife asked the king to give them names. The eldest son was born on a plate, so he was given the surname Pan; the second son was born in a basket, so he was given the surname Lan. Only the third son was not given a suitable surname, and it so happened that thunder rumbled in the sky, so he was given the surname Lei. Later, the youngest daughter grew up and married a brave soldier named Zhong, so she followed her husband's surname.

seclusion

n. 隐居；隔离

harmonious

adj. 友好和睦的；和谐的

From then on, the people with the surnames Pan, Lan, Lei and Zhong multiplied into a large ethnic group, and all of them worshiped Pan Hu as their first ancestor and their protector.

TIPS: The story has different versions which are much the same, and it is passed down among the ethnic groups of Yao, Miao and Li in southern China. People honor Pan Hu with the title King Pan. The word "Pan Hu" is pronounced as "Pan Gu". This fantasy myth about the origin of Pan Gu fills the **margin** of the *Hongmeng* Era before he created the heaven and the earth, signifying that he is the common old ancestor of the Chinese nation.

margin
n. 空白

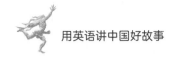

盘古开天辟地

相传万物之初，天地混沌一团，看上去像个大鸡蛋。盘古就孕育在这个"大鸡蛋"里面，悄悄地生长着。

过了一万八千年，盘古在"大鸡蛋"中生长"成熟"了。他猛然睁开了眼睛，发现四周漆黑一片，就抡起手中的大斧子，在"大鸡蛋"里一阵乱砍。

随着一声声巨响，混沌的"大鸡蛋"被劈开了，其中一股清而轻的阳气缓缓上升，变成了天空；浊而重的阴气渐渐下沉，变成了大地。因为盘古的一顿乱砍，宇宙从此不再是混沌一团，而有了天地和上下之分，顿时清爽多了。

盘古担心天与地会重新合拢到一起，于是伸出健壮有力的双臂撑着天，脚踩着地，屹立其间，不让天地重合。盘古就这样支撑着天地，每天长高一丈，天空也就随之升高一丈，大地也随之增厚一丈……

如此又经过了一万八千年，此时天已变得极高，地也变得极厚了，而盘古也长成了长达九万里的巨人。他犹如一根高大无比的擎天柱，直挺挺地支撑在天和地之间。在天地再也不可能重归于混沌的时候，盘古开天辟地的工程也总算完美地画上了句号。

在盘古开天辟地之后，世间才出现三皇（天皇伏羲、地皇女娲、人皇神农），也就是华夏文明的始祖。

【阅读小贴士】盘古是中国神话传说中的创世之神，其最早的相关文字记载出现在三国时期。今河南桐柏一带一直流传着盘古诞生的传说。2005年，河南省桐柏县被中国民间文艺家协会正式命名为"中国盘古之乡"。2006年10月30日，桐柏举办了"全球华人首次祭祀盘古大典"，并将每年农历九月初九定为全球华人祭祀盘古日。

Pan Gu Creating the Heaven and the Earth

According to legend, at the beginning of all things, the heaven and the earth were **chaotic** and looked like "a big egg". Pan Gu was conceived in the "big egg" and grew quietly.

Over the course of 18,000 years, Pan Gu grew "mature" in the enormous egg. When he suddenly opened his eyes, he found that it was dark around him, so he swung his big axe and **slashed** it in the "big egg".

With a loud bang, the chaotic "big egg" was split open, and a clear and light *yang qi* floated up to become the sky, while the dense and cloudy *yin qi* gradually sank down to become land. Pan Gu spilt *yin* and *yang* with his axe, so the universe was no longer in a chaotic mess, but a much fresher place, with a division of the heaven and the earth, as well as the upper and the lower.

Fearing that the heaven and the earth might be brought back together, Pan Gu stretched out his strong and powerful arms to support the sky and his feet to tread on the earth, standing in between. He supported the heaven and the earth in this way for 18,000 years. Every day both he and the universe grew—the earth grew ten feet thicker while Pan Gu grew ten feet taller…

chaotic

adj. 混乱的；乱糟糟的

slash

v. 劈，砍

After eighteen millennia, the sky had become extremely high and the earth had become extremely thick, while Pan Gu had grown into a 90,000-*li* giant. He was like a pillar of **immense** height, standing upright between the heaven and the earth. When it was no longer possible for the heaven and the earth to return to chaos, his work of creating the heaven and the earth came to a perfect conclusion.

It was only after Pan Gu created the heaven and the earth that there appeared the legendary Three Sovereigns (the Heavenly Sovereign or Fuxi, the Earthly Sovereign or Nüwa, and the Human Sovereign, Shennong), who were the earliest divine lords in Chinese cultural.

immense

adj. 极大的；巨大的

TIPS: Pan Gu is the God of Creation in Chinese mythology and legends, and was first recorded in the Three Kingdoms period. The legend of his birth has been passed down around Tongbai in Henan Province. In 2005, Tongbai County, Henan Province was officially named the "Township of Pan Gu in China" by the Chinese Folk Artists Association. On October 30, 2006, Tongbai held the "First Global Chinese Ritual for Pan Gu" and set the 9th day of the 9th month of the lunar calendar as the global Chinese ritual day for him.

盘古化生万物

盘古成功开天辟地后,便保持着头顶天、脚踏地的姿势屹立于天地之间。直到再次经过一万八千年的生长和变化,在天地变得与今天没有什么差别时,盘古很满意,也很累,他耗尽了最后一丝力气,"轰"的一声倒下,再也站立不起来了。

盘古的另一项事迹是在死后将自己的身体化作宇宙万物。盘古临死的时候:他口里呼出的气变成了耳边吹着的风和天上飘着的云,口中发出的声音变成了轰隆作响的雷霆;他的左眼变成了太阳,右眼变成了月亮,四肢五体则化成了大地的四极和五方的名山——东岳泰山、西岳华山、南岳衡山、北岳恒山、中岳嵩山;他的血液变成了滔滔江河,筋脉变成了山川道路,肌肉变成了沃土肥田;他的头发变成天上的星辰,身上的汗毛变成花草树木,点缀在山川和平原上;牙齿和骨头变成了金属和岩石,流下的汗水变成了润泽万物的清露和甘霖;就连寄生在他身上的各种小虫子,也在暖风吹拂下,变成生活在大地上的黎民百姓。

盘古为了一个美好世界的诞生,贡献了自己的一切。

【阅读小贴士】在中国古代神话的众多创世神中,盘古是唯一一位因创世而献身的神。同时,盘古化生万物,不仅反映了人类是自然的主人,也更体现了天人合一、人神合一、人与自然合一的东方生态哲学的思想光辉。

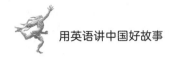

Pan Gu Giving Birth to All

After Pan Gu had succeeded in creating the heaven and the earth, he remained placing himself between them and pushing the sky away from land. After another 18,000 years of growth and change, when the heaven and the earth had become no different from today, he was very satisfied, but also very tired. Exhausting the last ounce of strength and **collapsing** with a loud bang, he could no longer stand up.

Another great deed of Pan Gu is that his body transformed into the universe after his death. As he was dying, his body began to transform: the last of his breath became the winds and the clouds; his voice became **the rumblings thunder**; his left eye became the sun; his right eye became the moon, and his four limbs and trunk became the four extremes of the earth and the famous Five Mountains—Mount Tai in the east, Mount Hua in the west, Mount Heng in the south, Mount Heng in the north, and Mount Song in the middle; his blood became the mighty rivers, his veins became the earth's arteries, his flesh became **fertile** lands; his hair and beard became the stars in the sky, his skin and body hair became the flowers and trees, dotting the mountains and plains; his teeth and bones became various metals and rocks, his sweat became

collapse

v. (突然) 倒塌

the rumblings thunder

隆隆的雷霆

fertile

adj. 肥沃的；富饶的

the dew and the rain that moistened all things; even the various small insects on his body reacted to the wind and turned into human beings.

He contributed everything he had to the birth of a better world.

TIPS: Among the many creator gods of ancient Chinese mythology, Pan Gu is the only one who **dedicated** himself to the creation of the world. At the same time, his creation of all things not only reflects that human beings are the masters of nature, but also reflects the ideological glory of the Eastern ecological philosophy, including the unity of heaven and man, the unity of god and man, and the unity of nature and man.

dedicate

v. 把……奉献给

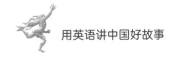

女娲创造人类

随着天地被开辟出来,世上有了日月星辰、山川河流、花草树木、飞禽走兽,但唯独没有人类。人类是从哪里来的?除盘古化生人类的说法外,在中华民族流传最广的便是女娲抟土造人的神话故事。

传说女娲是从大地里生长出来的女神,人首蛇身、神通广大。当她独自生活在世上时,感到孤单和寂寞,产生了仿照自己造人的想法。

女娲造人的传说有多个版本,大同小异。其中有一种说法是女娲嫌众神合作造人的速度太慢,就想出抟土造人的新办法。她将黄土加上水和成泥,在手中揉搓着,仿照自己捏成了一个小泥娃娃,然后她向泥娃娃吹了一口气。说来也奇怪,这个泥捏的小家伙一接触地面,就活了起来,跳跃着、欢呼着。女娲惊喜万分,将自己亲手创造的孩子取名叫"人"。

女娲想更快地造出更多的人,她把荆条编成的绳子放在黄泥里,抖动绳子将黄泥甩出去,无数的泥点落地后,立刻变成了一个个活泼跳跃着的小人儿。女娲就这样不知疲倦地忙碌着,一天又一天,用辛勤的劳动创造出无数的儿女,让大地上从此布满了人类的足迹。

【阅读小贴士】女娲是中国上古神话中的创世女神,被尊为始母神(中华民族的母亲)、华夏民族的人文始祖和福佑社稷的正神。女娲造人的神话故事,反映了中华民族传承不息的创新精神及华夏文明的起源。

Nüwa Creating Human Beings

As the heaven and the earth have been created, there are the sun, the moon, stars, mountains, rivers, flowers, trees, birds and animals, but no human beings. Where did the humans come from? Apart from the theory that Pan Gu gives birth to all things, the most popular myth among the Chinese is that the godness Nüwa creates human beings out of **clay**.

Legend has it that Nüwa was a goddess who grew out of the earth, with a human head and a snake body, and with great powers. When she was living alone in the world, she felt lonely and **isolated** and had the idea of creating human beings in her own image.

There are several versions of the legend that she creates human beings, all of which are similar. One of them is that she thought that the speed of the gods' cooperation in creating human beings was too slow, so she came up with a new way of molding them from clay. She mixed the yellow clay with water to make mud, **kneaded** it in her hands and made it into a small clay doll as if it were herself, then she blew on it. Strangely enough, as soon as the clay doll touched the ground, it **came to life**, jumping and cheering. She was so surprised that she named the children she had created with her own hands "Ren" (Ren

clay

n. 黏土；陶土

isolate

v. 使（孤立）；脱离

knead

v. 揉，捏

come to life

苏醒，变得活跃

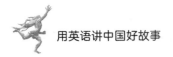

actually means "human being" in English).

    Nüwa wanted to create more human beings faster. She put the rope made of wattle in the yellow mud and shook the rope to throw the mud out. The **countless** mud dots fell to the ground and immediately became the little people jumping around lively. Day after day, she worked tirelessly and created countless sons and daughters with her hard work, and the earth was covered with human footprints from then on.

countles

adj. 无数的

TIPS: Nüwa is the Goddess of Creation in ancient Chinese mythology, and **is respected as** the Mother Goddess of the Beginning (the mother of the Chinese nation), the cultural ancestor of the Chinese nation and the god who blesses the land and society. The mythical story of her creation of human beings reflects the endless spirit of innovation of the Chinese nation and the origins of Chinese civilization.

be respected as

被尊为……

颛顼与共工争帝

相传4500年前,天帝颛顼与水神共工之间爆发了一场夺权大战。颛顼是黄帝的后裔,共工是炎帝的后裔。共工不服颛顼的统治,向天帝宝座发起挑战。颛顼大怒,一面召集诸侯疾速支援,一面亲自挂帅迎战,双方杀得天昏地暗。

共工长着人脸蛇身,统治着地面百分之七十的水域,他呼风唤雨,造成洪水泛滥,企图借洪水的力量打败颛顼。颛顼以洪水伤害生灵为由,得到诸神相助,在混战中杀死了共工的儿子,还用计烧死了共工的手下大将浮游和相柳,把共工逼退到西北方的不周山下。

不周山是一根撑天的巨柱,绝望的共工朝不周山撞去,只听"轰隆隆"一阵巨响,不周山被他拦腰撞断。他这一撞不仅撞破了天空,引发天河倾泻而出,人间泛滥成灾,而且把连接大地的绳索也给撞断了,导致拴系在北方天空中的太阳、月亮和星星向西滑动,意外地打破了颛顼将日月星辰固定在天空同一个地方的做法,解除了当时人们所遭受的白昼和黑夜不能交替所带来的痛苦。不周山倒塌后,还使东南大地塌陷,呈西北高、东南低的地势,引发百川之水往地势低的东南边流去,汇集成东边的海洋。

【阅读小贴士】共工和颛顼之战,其实质是权力之争。古人借共工怒撞不周山的后果来解释天象和地势,是以神话的想象力来解释自然力的生动写照,反映了古人探究自然奥秘的智慧。

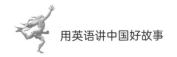

Zhuanxü and Gonggong Competing for the Throne

According to legend, 4,500 years ago, a great battle for power broke out between Zhuanxü, the Emperor of Heaven, and Gonggong, the God of Water. Zhuanxü was a **descendant** of Yellow Emperor and Gonggong was a descendant of Emperor Yan. Gongong was displeased with Zhuanxü's rule and challenged him for the throne of the supreme god. Zhuanxü was furious; he **summoned** his lords to support him at a great speed while taking charge of the battle personally. The two sides fought with each other to the death.

Gonggong, who had a human face and a snake body, ruled over 70 percent of the earth's waters and called the wind and rain to cause floods, trying to use the power of the floods to defeat Zhuanxü. Zhuanxü **cited** his use of floods to harm living beings as a reason, and with the help of the gods, he killed his son in a **melee**, and also used a trick to burn his generals named Fu You and Xiang Liu, he drove Gonggong back to the northwest, under Mount Buzhou.

The mountain was a huge pillar that held up the sky. The desperate Gonggong **butted** into Mount Buzhou, After a loud bang, the sky pillar collasped which caused great

descendant
n. 后代，子孙

summon
v. 召集；召唤

cite
v. 提及；列举

melee
n. 混乱

butt
v. 用头撞（顶）

disasters. Water flowed with no sign of abating, the world suffering from floods; he also broke the rope connecting the earth. This caused the sun, moon and stars tied to the northern sky to slide westwards, accidentally breaking Zhuanxü's practice of fixing the sun, moon and stars in the same place in the sky, relieving the people of the suffering caused by the inability to **alternate** day and night. The collapse and shaking of the mountain also caused the southeastern earth to collapse into a high northwestern and low southeastern terrain, causing the water for hundreds of rivers to flow to the southeast, where the terrain was low, and converged to form an ocean in the east.

alternate
v. (使)交替; 使(轮流)

TIPS: The battle between Gonggong and Zhuanxü is essentially a power struggle. But using the consequence of Gonggong's angry collision with Mount Buzhou to explain the **celestial** and **terrestrial** phenomena is a vivid portrayal of the power of nature explained by the imagination of mythology, reflecting the wisdom of the ancients in exploring the mysteries of nature.

celestial
adj. 天空的; 上天的

terrestrial
adj. 地面上的; 陆地的

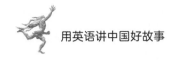

女娲补天

女娲在完成造人和为人类建立婚姻制度的心愿后,很有幸福感,觉得再也没有什么事值得她去忧心了。没想到共工怒撞不周山,把天空撞出了一个大窟窿,导致天河泛滥,给人间带来巨大灾难。女娲看在眼里,痛惜万分,发誓要把天上的缺口补上,却苦于找不到补天的办法。

一天,她梦见一位老者告诉她,昆仑山顶的五色宝石,若用大火炼化,可以拿来补天。女娲醒来,便日夜兼程前往昆仑山,寻找五色宝石。

当她来到昆仑山下时,只见昆仑山高耸陡峭,上山无路。她毫不退缩,披荆斩棘,与恶兽搏斗。其救苍生于水火的不屈精神,感动了山神,山神变出了一条通向山顶的道路,让她成功找到五色宝石。

女娲把这些五色宝石垒放在一起,用神火炼了九九八十一天,直到宝石炼成了熔浆,再用双手捧起熔浆去补天。眼看只要最后一捧熔浆就可以补好了,突然吹来一股奇异的大风,把女娲手中的五色石熔浆吹走了。女娲惊呆了,怎么办?只要天空还有裂缝,随时就会崩裂开来。眼见裂缝已经开始扩大,女娲来不及多想,快速将自己的身体熔化了,用自己熔化的身体,把天空的隙缝完全补上了。

洪水退去了,人们重回家园,大地生机勃勃,女娲却再也回不来了……

【阅读小贴士】女娲补天的神话故事,在中国家喻户晓。女娲作为人类之母,创造了人类,又为拯救人类牺牲了自己。女娲集中华美德于一身,人们永远怀念她。

Nüwa Patching the Sky

Nüwa was happy after completing her wish of creating human beings and establishing the institution of marriage for mankind, and felt that nothing was worth worrying about anymore. Unexpectedly, Gonggong hit Mount Buzhou in anger and knocked a big hole in the sky, causing the heavenly river to flood and bringing great disasters to the earth. She looked at it and **deplored** it, vowing to fill the margin in the sky, but struggled to find a way to patch the sky.

deplore

v. 强烈谴责

One day, she dreamed of an old man who told her that the five-coloured gems at the top of Mount Kunlun could be used to patch the sky if they were refined with a great fire. When she woke up, she travelled day and night to the mountain to find the gems.

When she arrived at the foot of the mountain, she saw that the mountain was so high and steep that there was no way up. She did not **flinch**, picked her pathless way and fought with evil beasts. Her **unyielding** spirit of saving the people in danger moved the mountain god to give her a way to the top of the mountain to find the gems.

flinch

v. 退缩，畏缩

unyielding

adj. 顽强不屈的

She put these gems together and refined them with divine fire for ninety-one days until they became **molten** slurry, and then picked up the molten slurry with both

molten

adj. 熔化的

hands to patch the sky. It was only a matter of time before the last handful of molten slurry would patch the sky, a strange wind suddenly came and blew them away from her hands. She was stunned, what should she do? As long as there were still cracks in the sky, the sky would **crumble** open at any moment. Seeing that the cracks had begun to widen, she could not think any further and quickly dissolved her own body, using her molten body to completely fill the margin in the sky.

The floods receded, the people returned to their homes and the earth came to life, but Nüwa could never return…

TIPS: The myth of Nüwa patching the sky is a household story in China. As the mother of mankind, she created human beings and **sacrificed** herself to save them. She combines the Chinese virtues in one and will always be remembered.

crumble

v. 粉碎；瓦解

sacrifice

v. 牺牲

神话故事

天女散花

相传盘古开天辟地后,让自己的儿子掌管天庭,人称玉皇大帝;让自己的女儿掌管百花,人称花神。天女散花的神话讲的便是花神的故事。

盘古在开天辟地时,耗尽了身体里最后一丝元气。他临终时,将一包百花种子交给女儿,对女儿说,带上这包种子先往西走二万二千二百二十二里,那里有一座净土山,取净土一担摊在天石上,把这百花种子种在净土里;然后往东走四万四千四百四十四里,那里有一潭不蒸不发的真水,取真水一担,浇灌百花种子,百花种子就会生根发芽;接下来再往南走六万六千六百六十六里,那里有一潭善水,取善水一担,喷洒花苗,花苗便会结出花骨朵儿;最后往北走八万八千八百八十八里,那里有一潭美水,取美水一担,滋润花骨朵。这样,就会开出百种花朵。盘古希望女儿种出美丽的鲜花,让芳香飘溢天上人间。

盘古死后,女儿牢记父亲的嘱托,先是往西走,取了一担净土,然后又分别向东、向南、向北走取来真、善、美三潭里的水,历经千辛万苦完成了父亲的临终嘱托。终于有一天,百花怒放,天庭瞬间变成了美丽的花园,很多地仙到天庭办事,看到天庭里的美景花香,都舍不得再回到人间,让玉帝很是苦恼。

花神得知哥哥的烦恼后,却笑了。她接下来的工作,正是要把鲜花撒向人间。玉帝要助妹妹一臂之力,唤来一百名仙女,封她们为百花仙子,任由花神调动。百花仙子在花神的安排下,手托花篮,穿梭在花园中,各自采下自己最喜爱的鲜花,采摘牡丹花的仙女就变成了牡丹仙子,采摘荷花的仙女就变成了荷花仙子,采摘了不同鲜花的仙女变成百名不同的花仙子。当她们将花篮装满时,花神一声令下:"把你们采来的花撒向人间吧。"

百花仙子飘向空中,将鲜花撒向人间。这些鲜花飘落九州,马上落地生根。从此，人间有了百花。

【阅读小贴士】天女散花讲的仍然是神造万物的故事，却有尽孝的美德和创造美的精神。人间的真、善、美只能生长在净土里，需要人们通过劳动去创造。

Heavenly Maidens Scattering Flowers

According to legend, after Pan Gu created the heaven and the earth, he put his son in charge of the heavenly court, known as the Jade Emperor, and his daughter in charge of the flowers, known as the Goddess of Flowers. The myth of the heavenly maidens scattering flowers is the story of the Goddess of Flowers.

When Pan Gu was creating the heaven and the earth, he used up the last ounce of energy in his body. When he was dying, he gave a packet of hundred flower seeds to his daughter and said to her, "Take this packet of seeds and go west for 22,222 *li*, where there is a mountain of pure soil, take a load of soil and spread it on a heavenly stone, and plant the seeds of flowers in the soil; then go east for 44,444 *li*, where there is a pool of true water that does not **evaporate**, take a load of it and water the seeds of hundred flowers, and the seeds will take root and **sprout**; then go south for 66,666 *li*, where there is a pool of good water, take a quart of it and **sprinkle** the flowerbeds with it, and the flowerbuds appeared in them; then go north for 88,888 *li*, where there is a pool of beautiful water, take a quart of it and nourish the flower buds. In this way, hundred kinds of flowers will blossom." He hoped that his daughter would grow beautiful flowers and let the fragrance **waft** over the

evaporate

v. (使) 蒸发; 挥发

sprout

v. 发芽; 生长

sprinkle

v. 撒; 洒

waft

v. 飘荡

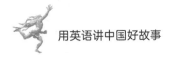

heaven and the earth.

After Pan Gu's death, his daughter remembered the entrust. She first went west and fetched a quart of pure soil, and then went east, south and north to fetch water from the three pools of truth, goodness and beauty respectively, and fulfilled her father's dying entrust after a great deal of hardship. Finally, one day, hundreds of flowers bloomed and the heaven instantly turned into a beautiful garden. Many earth immortals went to heaven on business, they saw the beautiful flowers and smelt the fragrance in it. They could not bear to return to earth, which made the Jade Emperor **distressed**.

However, the goddess of flowers smiled when she heard of her brother's troubles. Her next job was precisely to spread the flowers on the earth. The Jade Emperor wanted to help his sister by summoning a hundred fairies and crowning them as the Flower Fairies mobilized by his sister. Under the arrangement of the God of Flower, the fairies put flower baskets in their hands, went through the garden and picked their favourite flowers. The fairies who picked peony flowers became Peony Fairies, those who picked lotus flowers became Lotus Fairies, and those who picked different flowers became the hundred different Flower Fairies. When they had filled their baskets with flowers, the goddess gave a command, "Scatter the flowers you have picked to the earth."

The hundred flower fairies floated into the air and scattered the flowers to the world. These flowers floated

distressed

adj. 忧虑的；苦恼的

down and immediately took root on the ground. From then on, there have been hundreds of flowers on the earth.

TIPS: "Heavenly Maidens Scattering Flowers" still describes the story that the gods create all things, but it reflects the virtue of dutifulness and the spirit of creating beauty. The truth, goodness and beauty of mankind can only grow in the pure soil and be created through labour.

伏羲画卦

传说很久以前,在遥远的西北方,有个叫"华胥氏之国"的地方。一天,有一位叫华胥氏的美丽姑娘独自出去玩耍,她来到一片风景优美的大沼泽,这里被人称为雷泽。她发现在雷泽的边上,有一个巨大无比的脚印。受好奇心的驱使,这位姑娘踩上了雷神的大脚印,于是便有了身孕,十二年后生下一个儿子,他便是华夏民族人文先始、三皇之首伏羲。

伏羲是雷神的儿子,长着人头蛇身,能够自由地登着天梯上天下地,从小对大自然充满好奇和探索之心,经常盘坐山巅,仰观日月星辰,俯探山川河流,寻找他们的变化和法则,思考人与自然相处之道。

一天,伏羲正在山巅冥想,一声巨响把他惊醒,只见眼前闪出一派美妙的幻境:渭河水面上空飞来一匹龙马,悠悠然直落到河心的巨石上,龙马身上长有闪闪发光的奇妙花纹。伏羲凝视着,只见巨石也随之幻化为立体太极图案,阴阳缠绕、光辉四射。这幅太极神图,深深印入伏羲的脑海里,让他猛然顿悟了天人合一的密码:原来天地唯阴阳而已。

伏羲在神灵点化之下,便画出了八卦,用八种符号代表天、地、雷、风、水、火、山、泽等八种天象和地貌。八卦成列的基础是易象,重卦的基础则在于爻变,每一卦形代表一定的事物。"乾"代表天,"坤"代表地,"坎"代表水,"离"代表火,"艮"(gèn)代表山,"震"代表雷,"巽"(xùn)代表风,"兑"代表泽。八卦就像八只无形的大口袋,把宇宙万物囊括其中,互相搭配又变成六十四卦,用来象征各种自然现象和人事现象,造福民生。

【阅读小贴士】伏羲根据阴阳变化之理,创制了八卦,开启了中华民族的文化之源。八卦,即以八种简单却寓意深刻的符号来概括天地之间的万事万物,是中国古人认识世界时对事物的归类,也是中国古老文化的深奥概念,蕴含着解释自然、社会现象的深邃哲理。

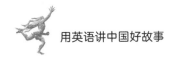

Fuxi Inventing the Eight Trigrams

According to Chinese mythology, in the far northwest, there was a place called the "Land of Huaxu". One day, a beautiful girl called Huaxu went out to play alone, and she came to a big **swamp** with beautiful scenery, which was known as the thunder swamp. She found a huge footprint on the edge of the swamp. Curiosity led the girl to tread in the huge footprint of the God of Thunder and she became pregnant. She gave birth to a son after twelve years of pregnancy. The son was Fuxi, who was counted as the first of the mythical Three Sovereigns in ancient china.

Fuxi was the son of the God of Thunder, with a human head and a snake body, and was able to climb up and down freely by the heavenly ladder. He grew up with a curious and exploratory mind for nature, often sitting on top of mountains, looking up at the sun, moon and stars, looking down at mountains and rivers, searching for their changes and laws, and **contemplating** the way for man to get along with nature.

One day, when he was **meditating** at the top of a mountain, he was awakened by a loud bang. He saw a wonderful vision that a dragon-like horse was flying above the Wei River and landing leisurely on a **boulder** in the centre of the river; the dragon-horse was covered with

swamp
n. 沼泽

contemplate
v. 考虑；思量

meditate
v. 冥想；沉思

boulder
n. 巨石；漂砾

the strange shining patterns. As he gazed at it, he saw the boulder transform into a three-dimensional Tai Chi pattern, with the entwining of *yin* and *yang*, glowing in all directions. The divine diagram of Tai Chi was deeply imprinted in his mind and made him realize the code of the unity of heaven and man: *yin* and *yang* are the only things in heaven and earth.

With the divine enlightenment, he created the Bagua or Eight Trigrams—eight symbols to represent the eight celestial and terrestrial phenomena of heaven, earth, thunder, wind, water, fire, mountain and marshland. The Eight Trigrams were arranged on *yi*-image, and the double sets symbols are based on the line changes, each representing a certain thing. "Qian" represents heaven, "kun" represents earth, "kan" represents water, "li" represents fire, "gen" represents mountain, "zhen" represents thunder, "xun" represents wind and "dui" represents marshland. The Eight Trigrams are like eight large and invisible pockets that encompass all things in the universe, and they are matched with each other to form the sixty-four divinatory symbols, which are used to symbolize various natural and human phenomena for benefiting the people.

TIPS: According to the theory of *yin* and *yang* changes, Fuxi created the Eight Trigrams, which initiated the origin of Chinese culture. It uses eight simple but profound symbols to summarize everything in heaven and earth. They are the categorization of things in the ancient Chinese understanding of the world, as well as the **esoteric** concepts of ancient Chinese culture, containing the profound philosophies to explain natural and social phenomena.

esoteric
adj. 深奥的；难领略的

伏羲降龙

伏羲发明了占卜八卦，那些将要发生的大事，他都能事先推算出来。

一天，伏羲在八卦台上掐指一算，拿起青龙拐杖，大喝一声："变！"青龙拐杖瞬间变成了一条青龙，伏羲骑上青龙腾飞而去。

原来，西北方的大山里有个深水潭，是人们做饭、洗衣、浇地等一切用水的来源。忽然一天夜里，狂风大作，一条黄龙从别处飞过来，钻进了深潭，饿了就钻出水面，不论是人还是牲畜，都不放过，张口就吃，吃饱了又躲进深潭里，吓得人们纷纷逃命。

伏羲推算出此事，就骑着青龙来到深潭边，准备降服黄龙。伏羲从身上掏出一个小铜锅，用火石打着火，烧着柴草，不到一个时辰，就把深潭里的水烧干了。黄龙熬不住了，变成小老头，拄着拐杖找伏羲拼命。伏羲喝斥黄龙认罪，黄龙现出了原形，张牙舞爪，口吐黑气，直向伏羲扑了过来。伏羲拿起青龙拐杖迎了上去，一拐杖打在了黄龙身上，黄龙顿时皮开肉绽，鲜血直流。黄龙仓皇往东逃窜，拱到了东边的大海里。

相传黄龙逃跑经过的地方，地面被拱出了弯弯曲曲的通道，后来就变成了黄河。

【阅读小贴士】伏羲是古代传说中的华夏民族的人文先始，也是中国古籍中记载的最早的王，同时还是中国医药鼻祖之一。伏羲降龙的故事体现了伏羲有一颗惩恶扬善、爱民如子之心。

Fuxi Subduing the Dragon

Fuxi invented and created the divination and eight divinatory symbols, so he could predict in advance all the events that would happen.

One day, he was on a divination platform for a prediction, picked up a green dragon walking stick and shouted, "Change!" The stick instantly changed into a green dragon, on which he mounted and flew away.

It turned out that there was a deep pool in the mountains in the northwest, which was the source of all water for people to cook, wash and water their land. Suddenly, one night, the wind blew up and a yellow dragon flew over from somewhere else and **burrowed** into the deep pool. When the dragon was hungry, it burrowed out of the water and ate both people and livestock. It ate at its fullest and then hid in a deep pool, scaring people into running for their lives.

When Fuxi **deduced** this situation, he rode the green dragon to the deep pool and prepared to **subdue** the dragon. He took out a small copper pot from his body and used a flint to make a fire in order to burn wood and grass. In less than an hour, the water in the deep pool was boiled dry. The yellow dragon could not stand any longer and turned into a old man with a walking stick and approached

burrow

v. 挖掘；挖洞

deduce

v. 推断；演绎

subdue

v. 制伏；征服

神话故事

Fuxi to fight for his life. Fuxi scolded the yellow dragon for confessing its sins, but it emerged in its original form, with the teeth and claws open and the mouth breathing black air, and **lunged** straight at him. He picked up the green dragon walking stick and struck the yellow dragon with it. The yellow dragon's skin was instantly split open and the blood was pouring out. It fled to the east in hurry and arched into the sea to the east.

lunge

v. 刺；戳

It is said that where the yellow dragon fled and passed through, its body arched out into curved channels, which later became the Yellow River.

TIPS: Fuxi is the ancient legendary human ancestor of the Chinese nation, and is also the earliest king recorded in ancient Chinese texts, as well as one of the originators of Chinese medicine. The story of his **subjugation** of the dragon reflects the fact that he has a heart to punish evil and love the people as if they were his own children.

subjugation

n. 征服；镇压

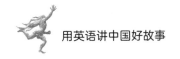

伏羲结网捕鱼

伏羲所处的时代，受自然界气候影响，人们主要靠打猎和采摘野果为生，没有稳定的食物来源。伏羲每时每刻都在想着如何改善人们的生活条件。

一天，伏羲来到野外，在暴雨来临之前，无意间看到一条又大又肥的鲤鱼跳出水面。他想如果人们可以抓鱼来吃，不是也可以填饱肚子吗？想到就去做，伏羲马上下河捉鱼，好不容易才抓到一条，拿回去用火烤了，分给人们吃。大家都被鱼的美味惊住了，纷纷请教伏羲抓鱼的办法。可如果人们都跑到河里抓鱼，不仅效率低下，而且惊扰了龙王的生活，龙王不许人们再下水捉鱼怎么办？

又一天，伏羲看见树枝中间有个蜘蛛在结网。一会儿，蚊子、苍蝇等飞过来，都粘在网上动不了，成了蜘蛛的美食。伏羲眼前一亮，上山找了一些葛藤编出一张大网，然后他把网放到河里，隔了一会儿，再把网提上来，他惊讶地发现网里有好多活蹦乱跳的鱼。这比下水徒手捞鱼省事又省力多了。

伏羲高兴极了，他把结网捕鱼的方法教给众人，人们争先恐后地学习并传承下去，这个方法非常好用，一直流传到今天。

【阅读小贴士】结网捕鱼这个故事，体现了伏羲爱观察、勤思考和亲力亲为的实干精神。正是有了这种精神，伏羲一生有很多发明创造，如发明八卦、创造文字、驯养野兽、火烤食物等。

Fuxi Fishing with a Net

There was no stable source of food due to the natural climate in Fuxi's time. People lived mainly by hunting and picking wild fruits. Fuxi spent every moment thinking of ways to improve the living conditions of the people.

One day, he went out into the wilderness and before the rain burst, he happened to see a big and fat carp jumping out of the water. He thought if people could catch fish to eat, wouldn't they be able to fill their stomachs? When he thought of it, he did it. He immediately went down to the river to catch fish, and with great difficulty he caught one, took it back and **roasted** it over the fire and distributed it to the people. Everyone was amazed by the deliciousness of the fish and asked him for advice on how to catch it. However, when people went into the river to catch fish, they were not only **inefficient**, but also disturbed the life of Dragon King, who forbade them to go into the water to catch fish. How would his children be able to eat?

Another day, he noticed a spider making a net in the middle of a tree branch. After a while, mosquitoes and flies flew over, but they were stuck to the net, becoming the food of spiders. He was enlightened and gathered up a bundle of wild reeds, wove them into a large net, ran down to the river bank, and threw his net in. After a while,

roast

v. 烤

inefficient

adj. 效率低；浪费的

he **hauled** it in and was shocked at how many fish were jumping in his net. It was much less work and effort than going into the water and catching fish by hand.

Delighted with his catch, Fuxi taught the people how to catch fish with a net, and they were eager to learn and replicate it. The way has worked well, so it has been passed down to the present.

TIPS: The story of fishing with a net is a reflection of Fuxi practical spirit of observation, diligent thinking and hands-on work. It is with this spirit that he made many inventions throughout his life, such as creating the Eight Trigrams, writing system and cooking, the **domestication** of wild animals.

haul
v. 拖，拉

domestication
n. 驯养；驯化

神话故事

火的"诞生"

从古至今,火在人们心中一直占据着非常重要的位置;火的发现亦是世界神话中普遍存在的主题。

远古时代,人们还不知道有火,也不知道如何用火。到了夜晚,一片漆黑,野兽的吼叫声时断时续,人们蜷缩在一起壮胆取暖,还要派人巡逻,防止野兽偷袭。由于没有火,人们只能吃生冷的食物,经常生病,寿命也不长。

一天,山林里下了一场雷雨。随着"咔"的一声,雷电劈在大树上,瞬间燃起了熊熊大火。人们吓得四处逃散,生怕大火会像"野兽"一样追过来伤害他们。

大火烧了一会,又被雷雨浇灭了。夜幕降临,逃散回来的人们聚在一起,惊恐地看着不远处燃烧未尽、仍在闪着火光的大树,不知如何是好。有个勇敢聪明的年轻人,发现燃烧的大树周围被照亮了,就好奇地向火靠近、再靠近。他突然发现离那棵燃烧的大树不远处,有一头被烧死的野兽,这时他才意识到:野兽可能也怕这个发亮的东西。他再次勇敢地向燃烧的大树走去,越靠近大树,越感到有一股热浪扑面而来,这种感觉让他舒适极了。他为自己的发现而兴奋不已,于是向伙伴们发出呼唤:"快来呀,这一点也不可怕,离它越近的地方越暖和啊!"

人们都信任这位年轻人,因为他总能给大家带来惊喜和解决难题的办法。于是,跑过来的人们紧跟年轻人的步伐,走向那头被烧死的野兽,他们闻到了阵阵香味,怎么回事?大家向年轻人投去询问的眼神。只见年轻人思索了一下,便蹲下身去,观察、摆弄着烧焦的野兽肉,原来是一只羚羊,他从羚羊身上撕下一块烧熟的肉,放进口中慢慢嚼食,他尝到了从未吃过的美味,立即招呼大家过来一起试吃。人们聚到火边,分吃烧过的羊肉,享受着上天赏赐的美味大餐。

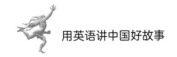

【阅读小贴士】故事讲述的是远古人类善于观察,偶然间发现了自然火。火给人类带来的神秘、温暖和美味,促使人类去思考火这种自然现象,并利用自然火来改善人类的生存环境,这将给人类命运带来革命性的转折。

The Discovery of Fire

Since ancient times, fire has always occupied a very important position in people's mind. The discovery of fire is a widespread motif in worldwide mythology.

In ancient times, people did not know about fire, or the way to use it. At night, when it was dark and the roar of wild animals was intermittent, people **huddled** together to **embolden** and keep warm, except for some ones being sent out to prevent wild animals from sneaking up on them. Without fire the people had to eat raw and cold food, so they would often get sick and live short lives.

One day, there was a thunderstorm in the forest. With a "click", lightning struck a tree and instantly a big fire started. The people fled in fear that the fire would come after them like a "wild animal".

The fire burned for a while and was **doused** by a thunderstorm. As night fell, the people who had fled gathered together and looked in horror at the burning trees. The trees still **glowed with** fire, not far away. They didn't know what to do. One brave and clever young man, noticing that the area around the burning tree was **illuminated**, approached the fire with curiosity and drew closer. He suddenly noticed a burnt beast who had died not far from the burning tree, and that's when he realized:

huddle
v. (通常因寒冷或害怕) 挤在一起

embolden
v. 使增加勇气; 使更有胆量

douse
v. 熄灭; 浇灭

glow with
发光

illuminate
v. 照明

the beast might also be afraid of this glowing object. Once again he bravely made his way towards the burning tree and the closer he got to it, the more he felt a wave of heat hit him and the feeling was comforting. Excited by his discovery, he called out to his mates, "Come on, this isn't scary at all! The closer you get to it, the warmer you feel!"

The people trusted the young man because he always had a surprise and a solution to their problems. Therefore, the people who had come running followed the young man's lead towards the burnt beast, they smelt a fragrance. What was going on? Everyone cast an enquiring look at the young man. After thinking for a moment, the young man knelt down and observed the charred meat of the beast, which turned out to be an **antelope**. He tore a piece of the charred meat from the antelope, put it in his mouth and chewed it slowly, tasting something he had never tasted before. He immediately greeted everyone to come over and eat the meat together. The people gathered around the fire and ate the roasted mutton, enjoying the delicious meal that the gods had given them.

antelope

n. 羚羊；羚类动物

TIPS: The story is about ancient men who were observant and **stumbled upon** the fire of nature. The mystery, warmth and deliciousness that the fire brings to mankind prompt them to think about fire as a natural phenomenon and to use it to improve the living environment, which will bring a revolutionary turn in the destiny of mankind.

stumble upon

偶然遇到

神话故事

钻木取火

自从有了火,黑夜里人们看到了光明,感受到了温暖;有了火,野兽不敢轻易冒犯;有了火,人们吃得香了,生病的人也明显减少了。人们知道了火的可贵,于是决定把"火"保留起来。大家每天轮流守着火种,不让它熄灭。就这样,"火"为人们服务了很久。可一天夜里,守着火种的人不小心睡过了,树枝燃尽,"火"还是熄灭了。

重陷黑暗和寒冷中的人们感到特别痛苦,再次面对生冷食物,也难以下咽了!那位聪明的年轻人安慰大家:"还会再找到火的!"

年轻人也不知道要到哪里去寻找"火"。他是多么渴望再来一场雷雨啊。日有所思夜有所梦。这天夜里,他梦见一位神仙告诉他:"在遥远的西方,有一片神秘的燧木林,你如果不怕吃苦,就去那里寻找火种吧!"

年轻人被梦惊醒,决定马上出发。他跋山涉水,历尽千辛万苦,终于看到梦中的燧木林。他跑进这片神秘的燧木林里,可是这里没有阳光,不分昼夜,四处一片黑暗,根本没有火!年轻人在黑暗中摸索前行,仿佛永远也走不到燧木林的尽头,也没有发现哪儿有一点点火光。这一天,他走累了,靠在一棵燧木树下休息。突然,他的眼前有亮光一闪,又一闪。年轻人立刻站起来,四处寻找光源。这时,他发现在不远处的燧木树上,有几只大鸟正在用短而硬的喙啄树上的虫子。每啄一下,树上就闪出明亮的火花。

年轻人惊呆了,脑子里灵光一闪,立刻折了些燧木的树枝,用小树枝去"钻"大树枝,树枝上果然闪出火光,可是却不见着火。年轻人没有气馁,又找来各种树枝,不停地尝试。终于,树枝在冒烟后燃起了火。

就这样,年轻人为人们带来了永远不会熄灭的"火种"——钻木取火的办法。从此,人们再也不用生活在寒冷和黑暗中了。

由于钻木取火中的树木用的是燧木,于是人们便把发明人工取火技术

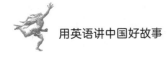

的年轻人尊为"燧",称其为"燧人氏"。人们相信燧,越来越多的人追随燧,很快便形成了以燧为首的远古人类氏族部落,这个氏族部落被后世形象地称为"燧明国"。

【阅读小贴士】中华民族素有崇拜"鼻祖"的传统,人们拥戴发现火并发明取火技术的人为"燧皇",奉为火神或火祖。《尚书大传》将燧人氏、伏羲、神农称为"三皇"。所谓"三皇",其实是原始社会为人类做出巨大贡献的部落领袖。

Drilling Woods for Fire

With fire, people could see light and feel warmth in the dark; with fire, wild animals did not dare to offend; with fire, people ate better and fewer people were sick. The people knew how valuable fire was and decided to reserve the "fire". Every day they took turns to keep the fire alive and not to let it go out. In this way, the "fire" served the people for a long time. One night, however, the man who was guarding the fire accidentally **overslept** and the branches burned out, finally the "fire" went out.

After being trapped in the darkness and cold, the people felt especially miserable and could hardly eat the cold food again! The wise young man reassured everyone, "We will find fire again!"

The young man didn't know where to look for "fire" either. How he longed for another thunderstorm. He was thinking about it all the day and dreaming about it at night. That night, he dreamed that an immortal told him, "In the far west, there is a mysterious forest of **flint**, if you are not afraid of hardships, go there and look for fire!"

Awakened from his dream, the man decided to set off at once. He travelled over the mountains and through all the hardships to finally see the flint woods of his dream. He ran into this mysterious flint forest, but there was no

oversleep

v. 睡过头

flint

n. 燧石；火石

sunlight, but darkness anywhere, no day or night, no fire at all! The young man **groped** his way through the darkness, as if he would never reach the end of the flint wood, nor did he find the slightest glimmer of fire anywhere. One day, when he was tired of walking, he leaned against a flint tree to rest. Suddenly, there was a flash of light before his eyes, and then another. The young man immediately stood up and looked around for a source of light. At that moment he noticed some large birds in a flint tree not far away, pecking at the insects on the tree with their short and hard beaks. With each peck, bright sparks flashed from the tree.

grope

v. 摸索；探寻

The man was so stunned that he came up with an idea in his head. He immediately broke some flint branches and used the smaller branches to "drill" the larger ones. A firelight did flicker from the branch, but there was no fire. Bracing himself, he found various branches to try many times. Finally, the branch burst into flames after smoking.

Thus, the young man brought to the people a fire that would never go out—a way to drill woods for fire. From then on, people no longer had to live in cold and fear.

The trees used in drilling for fire are made of flint woods, so the young man who invented the technique of making fire by drilling woods was called Suiren-shi (in which sui literally means "flint", ren means "human being", and shi here is a respectful address of ancient heroes). People believed Sui, and more and more people followed him, soon forming a **clan** of ancient humans headed by Sui, which has come to be known as the "State

clan

n. 氏族

神话故事

of Sui Ming".

TIPS: The Chinese people have a tradition of worshiping their "ancestors". The person who discovered fire and invented the technique of taking fire is known as "Sui Huang", and is worshiped as the God of Fire or Ancestor of Fire. In the *Standard Interpretation of Shangshu*, Suiren, Fuxi and Shennong are referred to as the Three Sovereigns, who were actually tribal leaders who made great contributions to mankind in **primitive** society.

primitive

adj. 原始的

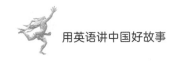

击石取火

燧人氏发明钻木取火之后，极大地改变了人类生存的环境。人们开始用火烧熟食物，用火取暖，用火驱赶毒虫猛兽。可是，有一个问题始终困扰人们，就是如何保存火种。特别是雨天雨季，火种不好保存，人们用潮湿的燧木来取火也难上加难。因此，那时部落里有专门负责保存火种的火正官。

传说火神重黎是发明击石取火的人。

当重黎还是个十多岁孩子的时候，他特别喜欢玩火，因为他是氏族首领的儿子，也就没人敢阻碍他每天围着"火"转。只要是与"火"有关的事，他都爱管，渐渐成了管"火"高手。无论是管理火种，还是钻木取火及烧烤食物，谁也比不了他。后来，他的父亲干脆让他管理部落的火种。

有一天，在长途迁徙中恰逢大雨，重黎随身携带的火种熄灭了。如果失去了火种，人们就无法生火做饭、取暖。重黎着急万分，想用钻木取火的方法取火，可是他带来的木柴全是湿的，钻了很长时间，也未钻出火星。眼看天要黑了，重黎累得满头大汗，毫无结果，一气之下，便把手里的钻头狠狠地扔了出去。不料，钻头碰击在石洞的岩石上，溅出很多的火星。重黎喜出望外，他找来好多石块在大青石上用力敲击着，只见火星不断飞溅。他连忙拿来易燃的芦花，靠着芦花敲击两块山石，很多的火星落在芦花上，芦花居然冒起了火苗。

重黎兴奋极了，人们也欢呼起来，祝贺重黎找到了更快捷的取火方法——击石取火。帝喾封重黎为"火正官"，赐名祝融，后世尊其为火神。

【阅读小贴士】重黎,又名祝融,相传是黄帝后裔高阳氏的玄孙。他不仅发明了击石取火的方法,而且还在黄帝与蚩尤大战中发明了火攻战法,在黄帝打败蚩尤的战争中立下大功。

祝融在中国传统文化中被尊为最早的火神,象征着我们的祖先用火照耀大地,带来光明。2021"中国航天日"启动仪式上,我国首辆火星车被命名为"祝融号",寓意点燃我国星际探测的火种,指引人类对浩瀚星空、宇宙未知的接续探索和自我超越。

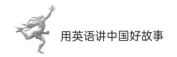

Striking Stones for Fire

After the invention of drilling woods for fire by Suiren, the environment of human existence was greatly changed. People began to use fire to cook food, to keep warm and to drive away poisonous insects and beasts. However, there was one problem that always troubled people: how to preserve the fire. Especially on rainy days, it was not easy to preserve the fire, and it was even more difficult to drill the **damp** flint wood for fire. Therefore, the tribes had fire officials who were responsible for preserving the fire.

A legend has it that the God of Fire, Zhong Li, was the one who discovered the use of striking stones for fire instead of drilling woods for the fire.

When he was a teenager, he loved playing with fire. Since he was the son of the chief of the clan, no one dared to stop him from playing with it every day. As long as it had to do with fire, he loved it and gradually became a master of it. Whether it was managing fire, drilling woods for fire or grilling food, no one could beat him. Later, his father simply asked him to manage the tribe's **tinder**.

One day, during a long migration, it rained heavily and the tinder that he was carrying with him went out. Without the tinder, the people were unable to cook or

damp
adj. 潮湿的

tinder
n. 火种；易燃物

warm themselves. He was so anxious that he tried to drill woods for fire. But the firewood he had brought with him was all wet, so after drilling for a long time, no spark came out. It was getting dark and he was so tired and sweaty, but **to no avail**, that he threw the drill out of his hand in anger. Unexpectedly, the drill hit the rocks of the cave and spilled many sparks. He was overjoyed and found a lot of stones and pounded them on the boulder, only to see the sparks flying. He hastened to bring flammable reed flowers and struck two rocks with them. Many sparks fell on the reed flowers and they unexpectedly burst into flames.

He was excited very much. The people cheered and congratulated him for finding a quicker and more convenient way to get fire—by striking stones. At that time, Emperor Ku appointed him as the "fire official" and gave him the name Zhu Rong, which was later honored as the God of Fire.

to no avail
几乎毫无作用

TIPS: Zhong Li, also known as Zhu Rong, is said to be the grandson of the Gao Yang, descendants of Yellow Emperor. He not only invented the method of striking stones for fire, but also invented the method of fire attack in the battle between Yellow Emperor and Chi You, and made great contributions in the war in which Yellow Emperor defeated Chi You.

In traditional Chinese culture, Zhu Rong is revered as the earliest God of Fire, symbolizing our ancestors' use of fire to illuminate the earth and bring light. In 2021 China

Space Day launch ceremony, China's first **Mars Rover** was named Zhu Rong, symbolizing the ignition of the flame of interstellar exploration in China, guiding mankind in its successive exploration and **self-transcendence** of the vast starry sky and the unknown of the universe.

Mars Rover
火星探测器

self-transcendence
n. 自我超越

炎帝教民播百谷

炎帝与黄帝都是中华民族的始祖。炎帝又称神农氏。提起神农,大家都知道,他是远古时期伟大的农业之神,发明了许多耕田农具,教人们学会了种庄稼。

当时,人们靠打猎、捕鱼、采野果来吃饱肚子,常常发生争夺食物的战争,甚至丢失性命。神农想:要是有足够多的野果供人们采摘,那该多好!

于是,神农就把树木砍下来,发明了用于耕地的工具——犁、镢头之类,带领大家开垦荒地,准备播种百谷。

可是,要到哪里去寻找百谷的种子呢?传说有一天,天空中突然飞来一只全身通红的神鸟,嘴里衔着一株九穗的稻禾。神鸟仿佛是特意给神农氏送种子来的,在他的头顶上方盘旋,穗上的谷粒洒落到地上,神农将谷粒都拾了起来,播种在土里。

不久,种子发芽,大地长出了绿油油的禾苗。炎帝作为太阳神,给禾苗合理的光照时间和强度,很快庄稼长得又高又大。秋天百谷丰收,从此人们不再为食物而发愁了。

【阅读小贴士】炎帝发明了农用工具,又教会人们使用和播种五谷,被称为农业之神。这篇神话反映了人类由原始游牧生活向农耕文明转化的进程。

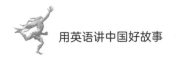

Emperor Yan Teaching People to Sow

Both Emperor Yan and Yellow Emperor are the originators of the Chinese nation. Emperor Yan, also known as Shennong, is known to everyone as the great God of Agriculture in ancient times, who invented many farming tools and taught people to sow crops.

At that time, people relied on hunting, fishing and picking wild fruits to feed themselves, and often fought over food and even lost their lives. Shennong thought: How wonderful it would be if there were enough wild fruits for people to pick!

Therefore, he cut down the trees and invented tools for ploughing the land—ploughs, **stiffeners** and so on—led the people to clear the land and prepare to sow hundred grains.

stiffener
n. 镢头

However, where could they find the seeds of the grains? According to legend, one day a red divine bird suddenly flew into the sky, carrying a nine-eared rice plant in its beak. The bird **hovered above** his head as if it had come specially to deliver seeds to him. The grains on the ears spilled onto the ground, and he picked them all up and sowed them in the soil.

hover over
盘旋于；威胁

Soon, the seeds sprouted and the seedlings grew green on the ground. As the Sun God, Emperor Yan gave the

神话故事

seedlings a reasonable amount of sunlight and they soon grew into tall and large crops. The harvest was abundant in autumn, and from then on, people were no longer worried about food.

TIPS: Emperor Yan invented agricultural tools and taught people how to use and sow the grains, and was known as the God of Agriculture. This myth reflects the transformation of mankind from a primitive **nomadic** life to an agrarian civilization.

seedling
n. 秧苗；籽苗

nomadic
adj. 游牧的

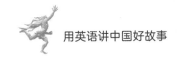

神农尝百草

上古时候，五谷和杂草长在一起，药物和百花缠在一起，哪些可以吃，哪些可以治病，谁也分不清。人类生存环境恶劣，面临着吃不饱、生病早逝两大威胁。爱民如子的炎帝神农氏，看在眼里，急在心头。他一边寻找可以用于种植的食物种子，教会人们播种农作物，一边寻找可以治病的药材，为人们减轻疾病的伤害。

有一天，神农到天帝花园采取瑶草（即灵芝），天帝得知他治病救人的志向后，把一条叫"赭（zhě）鞭"的神鞭送给他。这条神鞭能够帮助神农辨别草药：经过神鞭鞭打过的草药会自动呈现其自身的药性，例如有无毒性，寒性还是热性。

为寻找更好的草药，神农带着人们向西北方的大山出发，走了七七四十九天，来到层峦叠翠、长满奇花异草的大山谷旁。他用神鞭赶走了这里的虎豹野兽，历经千难万险，爬上高山去采药。每采一种草药，神农都要亲自尝试，并详细记下草药的药性和自己身体对药性的反应：哪些草是苦的，哪些是甜的，哪些能充饥，哪些能治病……都记录得清清楚楚。

有一次，他刚把一棵草放进嘴里，就说不出话来，感到天旋地转，然后一头栽倒。"他又中毒了！"一旁的人慌忙扶起神农，赶紧喂下随身带着的红灵芝解毒，他才活了过来。相传他曾在一天内中毒七十次，又被自己医好了。人们每天都在为他担心，却劝阻不了他。

神农尝完这山的花草，又去尝另一山的花草。他尝出了谷、麦、菽、粱、稻可以充饥，就叫人把种子带回去，让大家种植，这就是后来的五谷。七七四十九天后，他踏遍了这里的山岭。神农尝出了三百六十五种草药，写成了《神农本草经》。人们生病了就可以照此来采草药医治。

后来，神农在山上采药时，误尝了有剧毒的断肠草，再也没能把自己救回来。

【阅读小贴士】为了纪念炎帝神农尝百草、造福人间的功绩,人们奉他为"药王神",并建药王庙四时祭祀,把他尝药的地方取名为"神农架"。据说山西太原有个神釜冈,那里还存放着神农尝药时用的鼎;在咸阳山中,也可以找到当年神农鞭药的地方。

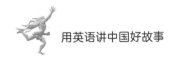

Shennong Tasting Hundreds of Herbs

In ancient times, grains and weeds grew together, medication and flowers **entwined**, so no one could tell which could be eaten or used for healing. The human was living in a harsh environment, facing the threat of not having enough to eat and dying **prematurely** from illness. Shennong, known as Emperor Yan, who loved the people like his sons, saw the situation and felt anxious. He searched for food seeds that could be used for planting and taught the people to sow crops, while at the same time searching for herbs that could be used to cure diseases and **alleviate** the damage caused by them.

One day, Shennong went to the garden of the Emperor of Heaven to take *yaocao* (ganoderma). When the emperor learned of his ambition to heal people, he gave him a divine whip called "**ochre whip**". This whip could help him to identify herbs: herbs that had been whipped by the divine whip would automatically show their own medicinal properties, such as whether they were poisonous, cold or warm?

In search of better herbs, he took the people to the north-western mountains and walked for seventy-nine days to a large valley with lush green hills, exotic flowers and rare herbs. He used his divine whip to chase away the

entwine

v. 盘绕

prematurely

adv. 早熟地；过早地

alleviate

v. 减轻；缓解

ochre whip

赭鞭

tigers and beasts from the area and climbed up the high mountain to gather herbs after numerous difficulties and hardships. For each herb he picked, he tried it himself, noting in detail the medicinal properties of the herb and his body's reaction to them: which herbs were bitter, which were sweet, which filled the stomach and which cured the sick. It's all recorded clearly.

Once, just after he had put a herb in his mouth, he was unable to speak, felt the sky spinning and then fell head over heels. "He's been poisoned again!" The men on the sidelines scrambled to help him up and hurriedly fed him the red ganoderma they carried with themselves to counteract the poison, and he came back to life. Legend has it that he was once poisoned seventy times in one day and was cured by himself. People worried about him every day, but could not **dissuade** him.

After tasting the flowers and herbs on this mountain, he went on to taste them on another mountain. He tasted grain, wheat, beans, sorghum and rice to **allay hunger**, so he asked people to bring back the seeds for everyone to plant, which later became the five grains. After forty-nine days, he walked all over the mountains and hills of this area. He tasted three hundred and sixty-five kinds of herbs and wrote the *Shennong Bencao Jing* (*Classic of Materia Medica*). When people were sick, they could follow this book to pick herbs for healing.

Later on, while picking herbs in the mountains, he mistakenly tasted the highly poisonous **gelsemium elegan**

dissuade

v. 劝阻

allay hunger

缓解饥饿

gelsemium elegan

断肠草

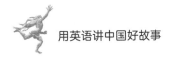

and never saved himself.

TIPS: In order to commemorate the achievements of Emperor Yan Shennong in tasting all kinds of herbs for the benefit of the world, people worship him as the God of Medicine, and build the temple of the God of Medicine to worship at all times. The place where he tasted medicine was named Shennongjia. It is said that there is a place called Shenfu Gang in Taiyuan, Shanxi Province, where the cauldron used by Shennong to taste medicine is still stored. In the mountains of Xianyang, the place where he whipped the medicine can also be found.

神话故事

神女瑶姬

关于神女瑶姬有很多美丽动人的传说,其中她帮助禹治水的故事,更是广为流传。

在这则故事里,传说神女瑶姬是西王母的第二十三个女儿,自幼跟三元仙君学道,有一身变化无穷的仙术,后被封为云华夫人。

瑶姬喜欢游玩,学道成功后,便从东海遨游回来。在经过巫山上空时,她看到这里山清水秀,便停留下来欣赏,恰遇大禹在此治水。

禹已在巫山脚下治水多年,虽历经千辛万苦,却没有多少进展。这片水域被十二条蛟龙霸占,它们常常出来兴风作浪,把这里变成汪洋一片,让百姓无法安居。大禹的治水工程,也一次次被恶龙掀起的狂风巨浪破坏。神女目睹恶龙的所作所为,感动于禹的治水精神,派六位侍女传授除魔法术,协助禹治水,把巫峡凿通,引洪水通向东海。

禹为感谢神女瑶姬的帮助,亲自登上巫山拜谢。瑶姬赠予禹一部治水用的黄绫宝卷,又命身边两位侍女继续帮助禹治水,疏导三峡水道。在神女的帮助下,禹终于赶走了恶龙,把这里十三年的洪水治理好了。

神女担心被打败的蛟龙还会回来作恶,就留在巫山,关注七百里三峡的行船安全,还派了无数神鸦在三峡上空巡飞,迎送来往的船只。神女太专心于三峡航道的安全了,在不知不觉地长久伫立中,把自己化成了一座秀丽挺拔的神女峰。她的侍从们也静静地守卫在神女的身旁,化作了一座座山峰,这就是我们今天所看到的巫山十二峰。

【阅读小贴士】这则故事反映了神女瑶姬乐于助人、惩恶扬善的精神。当地百姓还在飞凤峰山麓修建了一座神女庙,来祭拜神女。

The Goddess Yaoji

There are many beautiful and touching legends about the Goddess Yaoji, including the story of her helping Yu to control floods, which has been widely **circulated**.

In this story, it was said that Yaoji was the twenty-third daughter of the Queen Mother of the West. She studied with the Sanyuan Immortal Monarch since she was young and had an infinite variety of immortal skills. Later, she was **christened** Madame Yunhua.

She liked to travel, and after she succeeded in learning the Way, she came back from a trip to the East China Sea. When she passed over Mount Wu, she saw the picturesque scenery and stopped to enjoy the view, and happened to meet Yu here to control floods.

He had been controlling floods at the foot of Mount Wu for many years, but despite all the hardships he had gone through, he had not made much progress. The waters were **dominated** by twelve dragons, which often came out to make waves and turned the area into an ocean, making it impossible for the people to live in peace. His water management projects were also destroyed time and again by the fierce winds and waves whipped up by the evil dragons. While the goddess saw what the dragon had done, she was moved by his spirit of controlling floods and sent

circulate
v. 循环

christen
v. 命名为……

dominate
v. 支配；控制

six maids to teach him the magic of demon removal and to help him control floods by cutting through the Wu Gorge and diverting the floods to the East China Sea.

He was grateful for her help and climbed the mountain to thank her in person. She presented him with a yellow silk scroll for flood controlling, and ordered her two maids to continue to help him with the floods control and channeling of the Three Gorges. With the help of the goddess, he finally drove away the evil dragons and cured the floods that had **plagued** the area for thirteen years.

Worried that the defeated dragons would return to do evil, the goddess stayed at Mount Wu to keep an eye on the safety of ships travelling the 700-mile Three Gorges, and sent countless divine crows to fly over the Three Gorges to greet the incoming and outgoing ships. She was so preoccupied with the safety of the Three Gorges route that she transformed herself into a beautiful and upright peak as she stood unconsciously for a long time. Her attendants also stood by her side quietly, transforming themselves into the twelve peaks of Mount Wu that we see today.

TIPS: This story reflects the spirit of the Goddess Yaoji, who was willing to help others, punish evil and support goodness. The local people also built a temple to worship the goddess at the foot of Feifengfeng Peak.

plague

v. 折磨；烦恼

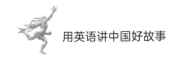

太阳神之女

炎帝的小女儿名叫女娃,漂亮、聪明,深得炎帝疼爱。

女娃非常敬佩父亲。那时候的炎帝很忙,每天忙着收集五谷种子、忙着上山采药。女娃已经很久没有见到父亲了,她很想念他,于是决定独自悄悄去寻找父亲,给他一个惊喜。

她的父亲是太阳神,她要到太阳每天升起来的东海边去寻找父亲,相信在那里一定能见到他。

一天清晨,东方的天空霞光四射,海面上波光闪闪,眼看着太阳就要冲出海平面与女娃相见了。突然间,东方的晨光消失了,海面狂风大作,巨浪向女娃迎面扑来,像张着大嘴的恶魔,瞬间吞没了女娃的船,女娃在水中挣扎着,呼喊着父亲,盼着太阳马上升出海面。

然而,她的父亲听不见她的呼救。此刻的炎帝神农氏,又因为尝百草而中毒了,他没有力气让太阳像平常一样冲破天边的乌云,按时升起来。

就这样女娃被无情的海水吞噬了……

【阅读小贴士】这则故事为"精卫填海"的前传,最早见于《山海经·北山经》。东晋大诗人陶渊明在《读山海经》诗中写道:"精卫衔微木,将以填沧海。"这是对精卫坚强不屈的意志、奋斗不息的精神最崇高的礼赞!

Daughter of the Sun God

The youngest daughter of Emperor Yan was called Nü Wa, a beautiful, intelligent girl who was loved by her father.

She admired her father very much. In those days, the emperor was very busy collecting seeds from the grains, going to the mountains to collect herbs. She had not seen her father for a long time. She missed him very much, so she decided to go alone and quietly to find her father and give him a surprise.

Her father was the Sun God, and she would go to the East China Sea where the sun rises every day to find her father, believing that she would be able to meet him there.

Early one morning, the eastern sky was glowing with **haze** and the sea was shimmering with waves, and it looked as if the sun was about to break out of the sea level to meet her. Suddenly, the morning light disappeared from the east, the gale was blowing on the sea, and the fierce waves came crashing down on the girl, like a demon with its mouth wide open, swallowing her boat in an instant. She struggled in the water, calling out to her father, hoping that the sun would soon rise above the sea.

However, her father could not hear her cries for help. At this moment, Emperor Yan Shennong, who had been

haze

n. 薄雾

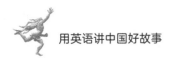

poisoned by the tasting of hundred herbs, did not have the strength to make the sun rise in time to break through the dark clouds in the sky.

And so, she was swallowed up by the merciless sea...

TIPS: This is the prequel of "Jingwei Filling up the Sea" which was first written in the *Shan Hai Jing* (*The Classic of Mountains and Seas*). Tao Yuanming, a great poet of the Eastern Jin Dynasty, wrote in his poem "Reading *Shan Hai Jing*", "Jingwei carries a pebble or twig in its mouth and unyielding to fill up the sea." This is the highest tribute to her strong and unyielding will and endless struggle!

精卫填海

炎帝得知女娃在东海溺水而死,悲痛欲绝。女娃死后变为彩首、白喙、赤足的小鸟,随父王狩猎,绕飞林中,悲鸣声似"精卫",炎帝举弓欲射,随从禀告:"这只鸟是陛下女儿女娃的化身!"炎帝心中一惊,放下弓箭,泪水盈眶,久久不能自已,许久之后才说:"就赐小鸟精卫之名吧!"

精卫久久盘旋不肯离去。炎帝作歌:"精卫鸣兮天地动容!山木翠兮人为鱼虫!娇女不能言兮吾至悲痛!海何以不平兮波涛汹涌!愿子孙后代兮勿入海中!愿吾民族兮永以大陆为荣!"

精卫听得父王"海何以不平"的歌词,于是决心填平大海。每日从西山衔来树枝和石子,填到东海里,往复飞翔,从不停息。后来,一只海燕飞过东海时无意间看见了精卫,海燕为精卫大无畏的精神所打动,就与其结成了夫妻,生出许多小鸟,雌的像精卫,雄的像海燕。小精卫和她们的妈妈一样,也去衔石填海。直到今天,它们还在做着这项工作。

【阅读小贴士】这是一则典型的变形神话,属于变形神话中"死后托生"神话,表达了先民对生死的一种理解。不仅如此,它还是复仇神话和女性悲剧神话的源头,具有丰富的文化内涵和研究价值。

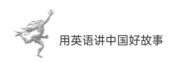

Jingwei Filling up the Sea

When Emperor Yan learned that his daughter had drowned in the East China Sea, he was **devastated**. After her death, Nü Wa turned into a small bird with a colored head, a white beak and bare feet, and accompanied her father on hunting. The bird flew around the forest, making the mournful cry of "Jingwei". When the emperor prepared to raise his bow to shoot, his attendant said, "This bird is the **incarnation** of your daughter Nü Wa!" He was shocked and put down his bow and arrow. Tears filling his eyes, he said he could not stop himself for a long time. After a long time he said, "Just give the name of the little bird 'Jingwei'!"

The bird hovered for a long time and refused to leave. The emperor composed a song, "Jingwei sings and the heaven and the earth are moved! The mountains and the trees are green and the people are fish and insects! I am saddened by the fact that my daughter cannot speak! Why is the sea so uneven and the waves so turbulent? May our children and grandchildren not go into the sea! May my nation always be proud of the mainland!"

Hearing the lyrics of her father's song "Why is the sea so uneven", she decided to reclaim the sea. Every day, she brought twigs and stones from the western mountains and

devastate
v. 摧毁；毁灭

incarnation
n. 化身

filled them into the East China Sea, flying back and forth, never stopping. Later, a sea swallow flew across the East China Sea and caught sight of Jingwei. Impressed by her fearless spirit, the swallow and Jingwei were married and had many children, among which the female looked like the mother and the male looked like the father. Like their mothers, the young birds went on to reclaim the sea with rocks in their mouths. To this day, they are still doing this work.

TIPS: This is a typical myth of **metamorphosis**, which belongs to the myth of "death and rebirth", expressing the understanding of the ancestors of life and death. It is also the source of the myth of revenge and the myth of female tragedy, and has a rich cultural connotation and research value.

metamorphosis *n.*
变形

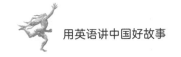

中央之神

黄帝，古华夏部落联盟首领，是中国远古时代华夏民族的共同祖先，五帝之首，被尊为中华"人文始祖"。

《史记·五帝本纪》记载："黄帝者，少典之子，姓公孙，名曰轩辕。生而神灵，弱而能言，幼而徇齐，长而敦敏，成而聪明。"其意思是：黄帝是有熊国国君少典的儿子，本姓公孙，名叫轩辕。相传他出生后不久就会说话，幼时聪明过人，长大后诚实勤奋，成年后见闻广博。传说他具有金、木、水、火、土五行中"土"的品德和特性，而土为黄色，故称"黄帝"。

在中国古代神话体系中，黄帝位为五帝之一的"中央之神"，即在他的四面各有一个天帝。东方的天帝是太皞（hào），由木神句（gōu）芒辅助他，手拿圆规，掌管着春天，是春神；南方的天帝是炎帝，由火神祝融辅助他，手拿杆秤，掌管夏天，是夏神；西方的天帝是少昊，由金神蓐（rù 褥）收辅助他，手拿曲尺，掌管秋天，是秋神；北方的天帝是颛顼，由水神玄冥辅助他，也就是海神兼风神的禺强，手拿秤锤，掌管着冬天，是冬神；黄帝则住在天的中央，成为中央的天帝和神，由土神后土辅助他，手拿一根绳子，监管着四面八方。

黄帝以统一华夏部落与征服东夷而统一中华的丰功载入史册。他在位期间，教化人民，播百谷草木，推广农耕，始制衣冠，发明车船，创制音律、创医学等。其医学著作被称为《黄帝外经》和《黄帝内经》。

【阅读小贴士】黄帝是以真实可考的历史人物为原型发展起来的神话人物。黄帝和炎帝时期逐渐形成华夏族，被视为华夏民族共同的祖先，所以中国人自称"炎黄子孙"。

God of the Central

Yellow Emperor, leader of the ancient Chinese tribal confederation, was the common ancestor of the Chinese people in ancient times, the first of the Five Emperors, and is **revered** as the "Ancestor of Humanity".

In *Five Imperial Biographies in Shiji*, "Yellow Emperor was the son of Shaodian, surnamed Gongsun, and named Xuanyuan. He was born with a divine spirit, being able to speak at an early age, young and favourable, grew up and became wise." The story goes that Yellow Emperor was the son of Shaodian, the ruler of the kingdom of Youxiong, whose surname was Gongsun and his name was Xuanyuan. It was said that he spoke soon after his birth, was clever as a child, honest and diligent after growing up, and knowledgeable as an adult. Legend has it that he had the virtues and characteristics of "earth", one of the five elements of gold, wood, water, fire and earth, and that earth is yellow, so he is called "Yellow Emperor".

In ancient Chinese mythology, Yellow Emperor was one of the Five Emperors, the "Central God", meaning that there was an Emperor of Heaven on each of his four sides. The eastern emperor was Taihao, assisted by the Wood God Goumang, who held a **round gauge** and was in charge of spring, he was the God of Spring; the southern

revere

v. 尊敬；崇敬

round gauge

圆规

emperor was Emperor Yan, assisted by the Fire God Zhu Rong, who held a scale and was in charge of summer, he was the God of Summer; the western emperor was Shaohao, assisted by the Gold God Rushou, who held a curved ruler and was in charge of autumn, he was the God of Autumn; the northern emperor was Zhuanxü, assisted by the Water God Xuanming, the Sea and Wind God Yuqiang, who held a weight and was in charge of winter, he was the God of Winter; Yellow Emperor lived in the centre of the sky and became the Emperor and God of the Central Heavenly, assisted by Houtu, the Earth God, who held a rope and supervised all directions.

Yellow Emperor went down in history for his great achievements of unifying the Chinese tribes and **conquering** the eastern barbarians to unify China. During his reign, he educated the people, sowed hundred grains and grasses, promoted farming, began to make clothes and crowns, invented chariots and boats, created music and rhythm, and created medicine. His medical works are known as Yellow Emperor's *Internal Canon of Medicine* and Yellow Emperor's *External Canon of Medicine*.

TIPS: Yellow Emperor is a mythological figure based on a real and **traceable** historical figure. The Chinese nation was gradually formed during Yellow Emperor and Yan Emperor period. The two emperors are regarded as the common ancestors of the Chinese nation, so the Chinese people call themselves "all children of Yan and Huang descendants".

conquer

v. 征服

traceable

adj. 可追溯的；可追踪的

炎黄之战

黄帝是位爱好和平的君王,但他一生却经历了两场大的战争,其中一次就是著名的"炎黄之战",又称"阪泉之战"。

传说黄帝和炎帝是同母异父的兄弟。黄帝是中央的天帝,炎帝是南方的天帝,兄弟俩本应井水不犯河水,各行其道、和平共处。

黄帝主张仁道,实行仁政,赏罚分明,官吏清正无私,百姓安居乐业,部落日渐兴盛。炎帝有称霸野心,为扩大势力范围,经常发起战争侵占弱小部落。那些弱小部落,不满炎帝霸道,都投靠了黄帝,黄帝势力因此加速扩大,炎帝对黄帝的不满也与日俱增。此时的炎帝又遇到内患,其部下蚩尤,野心勃勃,伺机向炎帝夺权。为实现自己称霸的野心,也同时转嫁内部矛盾,炎帝一箭双雕,向黄帝下了战书。

两位天帝开战,谁都想夺取胜利,战争非常惨烈。炎帝是太阳神,用的是火攻;黄帝是雷雨之神,以一场大雨应对,双方打了个平手。后来双方兵马在"涿鹿之野"大战一场,双方损失惨重。最后在"涿鹿之野"不远处的"阪泉之野",展开决战。黄帝以炎帝发动不正义的侵略战争为名,不但调遣了神兵神将,而且连虎豹豺狼、熊罴鹰雕等凶猛动物都带上了战场,终于打败炎帝。炎帝被迫退回自己南方的领地,偏安一隅,一蹶不振。黄帝从此拥有了对黄河流域的统治权。

【阅读小贴士】炎黄之战是神话传说中的一场旷日持久的大战,它反映了原始社会部族间的矛盾冲突。战争的胜负也说明了一个道理:得道多助,失道寡助。

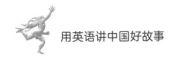

The Battle Between Legendary Emperors

Yellow Emperor was a peace-loving ruler, but he experienced two major wars during his lifetime, one of which was the famous Battle of Banquan, a series of battles between Emperor Yan and Yellow Emperor.

Legend has it that Yellow Emperor and Emperor Yan were half-blooded brothers. The former was the Central Emperor of Heaven and the latter was the southern Emperor of Heaven, and the two brothers were supposed to live in peace and not cross each other's paths.

Yellow Emperor advocated **benevolence** and practised benevolent rule, with clear rewards and punishments. The officials were clean and **impartial**. The people lived in peace and contentment. The tribes were increasingly prosperous. Emperor Yan had ambitions of domination and often waged wars against the weaker tribes in order to expand his sphere of influence. Those weak tribes were dissatisfied with his tyranny, so they all took refuge in Yellow Emperor. Yellow Emperor's influence therefore accelerated to expand, and the dissatisfaction of Emperor Yan with him was also growing day by day. At this time, Emperor Yan encountered internal problems, his **subordinate** Chi You, who was ambitious, was waiting for an opportunity to seize power from him. In order to

benevolence
n. 仁爱；善行

impartial
adj. 公正的

subordinate
n. 下属；部下

realize his ambition to dominate and to divert the internal conflicts, Emperor Yan killed two birds with a double-edged sword and sent a letter of war to Yellow Emperor.

The two Emperors of Heaven went to war, and the war was very fierce as both had to fight to win. Emperor Yan, the Sun God, who used fire to attack; Yellow Emperor, the God of Thunder and Rain, responded with a downpour and the two sides fought to a draw. Later, the two sides fought a battle at the open plain of Zhuolu, with heavy losses on both sides. The final battle took place at the open plain of Banquan, not far from the Zhuolu plain. In the name of the unjust war of **aggression** waged by Emperor Yan, Yellow Emperor not only deployed his divine soldiers and generals, but also fierce animals such as tigers, leopards, wolves, bears and eagles, and finally defeated Emperor Yan. Emperor Yan was forced to retreat to his own southern land and was left in a state of isolation and depression. Yellow Emperor henceforth had dominion over the Yellow River basin.

aggression

n. 挑衅；侵略

TIPS: The Battle Between Legendary Emperors is a mythical and long-lasting battle that reflects the conflict between tribes in primitive society. The victory or defeat of the war also illustrates the truth: A just cause attracts much support; an unjust one finds little.

蚩尤起兵复仇

"阪泉之战"后,蚩尤愤愤不平,多次挑唆炎帝,起兵复仇。炎帝感到力不从心,迟迟不动。蚩尤于心不甘,决定自己单干,还滋生了独霸天下的野心。

相传蚩尤面如牛首,背生双翅,骁勇善战,被尊称为"战神"。有一天,他在庐山脚下发现了铜矿,便收集起来做成了戈、戟、矛、弩等兵器,成为第一个用铜打造各种兵器的人。他觉得自己拥有非常厉害的兵器,加上具有呼风唤雨、兴云作雾等作战本领,能力不在黄帝和炎帝之下,而且还有八十一位兄弟辅助,就有了取代黄帝和炎帝的野心。一方面他软硬兼施,分化黄帝的下属,让他们作为内应;另一方面打着炎帝的旗号,招兵买马,伺机反叛。

蚩尤实力大增,野心暴涨,自称九黎部落首领,疯狂侵占炎帝地盘,逼炎帝让权,驱逐炎帝。炎帝向黄帝求助。此时黄帝也受到了来自蚩尤的战争挑衅。

黄帝不愿战争带给百姓伤害,多次派人劝说蚩尤,放弃战争,和平相处。蚩尤反而以为黄帝胆怯不敢应战,更加猖狂,逼黄帝一决高下。

黄帝派大将应龙出战,以大洪水向蚩尤汹涌扑去,却被蚩尤的大将风伯打败。风伯刮起狂风,把应龙发出的大洪水调转头来,向黄帝这边汹涌扑去。这始料未及的反转,让黄帝这边阵脚大乱。蚩尤乘机施法,一时天空扬沙、大雾弥漫,黄帝这边分不清方向,大败而归。

【阅读小贴士】黄帝战蚩尤的故事出自《山海经》。这是一场善与恶的战争,正义有时可能会迟到,但从来不会缺席。多行不义必自毙。

神话故事

Chiyou Starting a Revolt

After the Banquan Battle between Emperor Yan and Yellow Emperor, Chiyou was indignant and repeatedly provoked Emperor Yan to take revenge. The emperor felt overwhelmed and hesitated to take action. Chiyou was so upset that he decided to start a revolt, and developed the ambition to dominate the world.

According to legend, Chiyou had a human body, ox-headed with two wings on his back, and was so brave and resourceful in battle that he was revered as the God of War. One day, he found a copper mine at the foot of Mount Lushan and collected it to make weapons such as dagger-axes, halberds, spears and crossbows, becoming the first person to use copper to make all kinds of weapons. He felt that he had very powerful weapons, and with his ability to call the wind and rain and make clouds and fog, he was no less capable than Yellow Emperor and Emperor Yan and with the support of his eighty-one brothers, he had the ambition to replace the two emperors. On the one hand, he used both hard and soft **tactics** to divide the subordinates of Yellow Emperor so that they could act as internal agents; on the other hand, under the banner of Emperor Yan, he recruited troops and horses and waited for an opportunity to rebel.

tactic

n. 策略；战术

Chiyou, who had grown in strength and ambition, claimed to be the leader of the Jiuli tribes and frantically **encroached** on Emperor Yan's territory, forcing him to give up his power and expel him. The emperor turned to Yellow Emperor for help. At this time, Yellow Emperor was also provoked by a war from Chiyou.

encroach

v. 蚕食；侵占

Yellow Emperor did not want war to bring harm to the people, so he sent subordinates many times to persuade Chiyou to give up wars and live in peace. However, Ciyou thought that the emperor was too timid to fight in response and became more aggressive, forcing him to compete for championship.

The emperor sent his general Yinglong (literally means "Responding Dragon") into battle, lashing out at Chiyou with a great flood, only to be defeated by Chiyou's general Fengbo (the Wind Master). Fengbo blew the wind and made the great flood caused by Yinglong turn around to Yellow Emperor's side of the raging lunge. This unexpected reversal made the emperor's side **in disarray**. Chiyou took advantage of the opportunity to cast a spell, and for a while the sky was filled with sand and fog, the emperor's side was unable to distinguish its direction and finally came away with a big defeat.

in disarray

混乱

TIPS: The story of the battles between Yellow Emperor and Chiyou is from the *Shan Hai Jing*. This was a war between good and evil. Justice may sometimes be late, but it is never absent. Many acts of injustice will lead to death.

神话故事

黄帝备战蚩尤

初战失败后,黄帝及时总结经验教训,制定了多种御敌制胜的办法,在经过大小七十次战斗后,黄帝仍然未能战胜蚩尤。

正在黄帝一筹莫展之际,居住在玉山的大神西王母,派九天玄女前来助阵,为黄帝带来狐裘和灵符两件宝物。穿上西王母给的狐皮大衣,可以防身;佩戴上西王母画的灵符,可以在风雨云雾中不迷失方向。黄帝叹息道:"只有我一个人不受伤、不迷失方向,又怎么能打败敌人呢!"

在九天玄女的指点下,黄帝派人开采铜矿,用铜冶炼成一个个尖头的武器,绑到竹竿上,战时当作箭一样射出,用来破解蚩尤的大弩;黄帝的风后利用磁铁原理,发明了指南车,用于破解蚩尤的云雾,军队再也不会迷失方向。

黄帝考虑到蚩尤力大无穷,有腾云驾雾、呼风唤雨的本领,为防止他战败后从空中逃跑,黄帝事先安排能飞的应龙,在他逃跑时的路上拦截他;又从昆仑山召回女儿魃(bá,传说中的旱神),用她收云息雨的本领来破解蚩尤的呼风唤雨。可以说,经过几个月的周密筹划,黄帝已经做好了战胜蚩尤的准备,就等来犯之敌了。

【阅读小贴士】战争性质决定战争胜负,黄帝站在正义一边,不仅得到人民拥护,而且得到了西王母的支持,最终的胜利是必然的,但具体到每一场战争,又必须知己知彼,从失败中汲取教训,精心谋划,不打无准备之战。

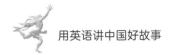

Yellow Emperor Preparing to Fight Chiyou

After losing the first battle, Yellow Emperor drew lessons from the experience and devised various ways to defeat the enemy. After seventy large and small battles, the emperor was still unable to defeat Chiyou.

When the emperor was at a loss, the Queen Mother of the West, who lived in the Mount Jade, sent the Empyrean Fairy to help him and brought him two treasures: a fox fur coat and a spiritual **talisman**. He can wear the coat given by the Queen Mother for protection and take the talisman drawn by her to keep from getting lost in the storm and clouds. He sighed to himself, "How can I defeat my enemies when I am the only one who does not get hurt or disoriented!"

With the guidance of the heavenly maiden, he sent subordinates to mine copper and smelt it into pointed weapons, which were tied to bamboo poles and shot like arrows in battle to break Chiyou's crossbows; his wife Wind Queen used the principle of magnetism to invent guiding cars to break Chiyou's clouds and fog, so that his army would never lose its way again.

Yellow Emperor thought that Chiyou was a powerful man with the ability to take to the air and call the wind

talisman

n. 护身符

and rain. To prevent him from escaping from the air after defeat, the emperor arranged for Yinglong, who could fly, to **intercept** him on his way to escape; he also recalled his daughter Ba (the legendary Drought Goddess) from Mount Kunlun and used her ability to collect clouds and rain to break Chiyou's ability to call wind and rain. It could be said that after months of careful planning, he was ready to defeat Chiyou and was waiting for the enemy to come.

intercept

v. 拦截；阻拦

TIPS: The nature of the war determines whether it is won or lost. Yellow Emperor is on the side of justice, not only **embraced** by the people but also supported by the Queen Mother of the West. So the ultimate victory is inevitable. But for each battle specifically, one must know his enemy, learn from defeat, plan carefully and not fight unprepared battles.

embrace

v. 拥戴

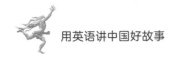
用英语讲中国好故事

黄帝大战蚩尤

蚩尤起兵向黄帝挑战以来,仿佛不费吹灰之力,打得黄帝节节败退,毫无还手之力。蚩尤以为他称霸天下的机会到了,亲自挂帅,要和黄帝决一死战。

蚩尤一马当先,手持长剑,冲向黄帝营地。黄帝这边也早早摆好阵势,佯装节节败退,将蚩尤军队引诱到阵中,突然吹响反击号角。蚩尤顿感大事不妙,连忙命风伯和雨师作法,掀起狂风和暴雨;黄帝的女儿魃立即作法接应,瞬间云消雨散,一滴水也没有落下。蚩尤勃然大怒,亲自作法,刹那间扬起一片浓雾;黄帝这边却推出一辆辆指南车,士兵紧跟其后,向着蚩尤的阵地包抄过来。一时间战鼓震天动地,呐喊声响彻山谷。蚩尤眼见大势已去,跳向空中想逃,谁知应龙早已在空中等候。蚩尤束手就擒,黄帝下令,杀蚩尤以谢天下。

黄帝战胜蚩尤之后,名声大振,各部落都拥他为"天子"。黄帝把首都设在部落根据地有熊(今河南新郑),建立黄帝王朝,下令今后各部落间的争执,不准用武力解决,改为向"天子"控诉,由"天子"为大家判断是非,由此确立了黄帝作为中华民族始祖的地位。

【阅读小贴士】中华始祖除了炎黄二帝外,还应该有蚩尤一个席位。炎、黄、蚩尤三大部落集团之间的战争,是那个时候推动社会进步的主要方式,蚩尤的失败不能掩盖他为中华民族的发展做出的巨大贡献。

神话故事

Yellow Emperor Fighting Chiyou

Since Chiyou rose to challenge Yellow Emperor, as if effortlessly, the emperor was defeated and **defenseless**. Chiyou thought he had a chance to dominate the world, and personally took command to fight the emperor to the death.

defenseless

adj. 无防备的

Chiyou took the lead, with his long sword in hand, and charged towards the emperor's camp. The emperor also set up a battle formation early, pretending to be in continuous defeat, and lured his army into the line, suddenly blowing the counter-attack horn. He felt that something was wrong, so he hurriedly ordered the Wind and Rain Masters to perform a spell to raise the wind and rain. The emperor's daughter Ba immediately performed a spell in response, and instantly the clouds and the rain disappeared without a drop of water falling. He was **furious** and did the spell himself, raising a thick fog instantly; however, the emperor launched guiding chariots, followed by his soldiers, towards his enemy's position. At that time, the battle drums shook the sky and earth, and the shouts resounded through the valley. Seeing that the momentum had gone, he jumped into the air and tried to escape, but Yinglong was already waiting in the air. He was captured and the emperor ordered that he should be

furious

adj. 暴怒的

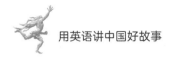

killed in order to apologize to the people of the world.

After Yellow Emperor's victory over Chiyou, his fame was so great that all the tribes embraced him as Tianzi (Son of Heaven). The emperor set up his capital in the tribal base of Youxiong (now Xinzheng, Henan Province) and established the dynasty of his time, ordering that future disputes between tribes should not be settled by force, but by complaints to Tianzi, who would judge right and wrong for everyone, thus establishing the status of Yellow Emperor as the founder of the Chinese nation.

TIPS: In addition to Emperor Yan and Yellow Emperor, there should also be a seat for Chiyou as the earliest ancestor of China. The wars between these three tribal groups were the main ways to promote social progress at that time, Chiyou's defeat cannot overshadow the great contributions he made to the development of the Chinese nation.

刑天舞干戚

蚩尤死后,又出现了一位敢于和黄帝对抗到底的人物,他是一位连名字都没有的巨人,因向黄帝发起挑战以失败告终,人们称他为"刑天"。"刑天"就是发誓杀天帝以复仇的意思。刑天与黄帝争位,他被斩去头颅后,仍然以双乳为眼,肚脐为口,再战黄帝。

刑天原是炎帝神农氏联盟部落中的一个臣子,长得高大威武,不仅勇猛善战,还特别喜欢音乐。在炎帝统治时期,他曾为炎帝作过《扶犁》《丰年》等乐曲,记录和歌颂了当时一段幸福美好的时光。

然而,岁月不饶人,年迈的炎帝自从败给黄帝后,灰心丧气,退回到南方,再也没有了与黄帝争霸的勇气。忠诚于炎帝的刑天为此愤愤不平,多次恳求炎帝联合蚩尤,夺取天下,无奈炎帝不为所动,以至蚩尤战败被杀的消息传来后,刑天怒火中烧。他左手持盾,右手执斧,独自向黄帝所在的中央天庭杀去,其排山倒海的气势,所向披靡,直杀到黄帝的宫门外,指名要与黄帝单挑独斗。

黄帝大怒,亲自迎战。于是,一场生死较量展开。两人从宫殿一直杀到郊外,又杀到炎帝的降生地常羊山,仍难分胜负。最后刑天不敌,被黄帝斩去头颅并埋在常羊山中。然而,刑天并没有因此死去,他似是把胸前的两个乳头当作眼,把肚脐当作口;两手拿着盾斧,愤怒地挥舞着,永不屈服。

【阅读小贴士】刑天英勇不屈的精神感动和鼓舞了一代又一代人。东晋大诗人陶渊明对刑天的这种精神大加赞颂,在《读山海经》中写道:"刑天舞干戚(干就是盾,戚就是斧),猛志固常在。"

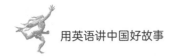

Xingtian Brandishing His Shield and Battle-ax

After the death of Chiyou, there was another figure who dared to fight against the supreme god to the end. He was a giant who did not even have a name: since the challenge to the Yellow Emperor ended in failure, people called him "Xingtian". The name means he swore to kill the emperor in order to take revenge. Xingtian continues to fight against Yellow Emperor even after his head being cut, using his nipples as eyes and his navel as mouth.

He was originally a minister of Emperor Yan Shennong's **alliance** tribe, tall and powerful, not only brave and resourceful in battle, but also particularly fond of music. During the reign of Emperor Yan, he composed music for him, such as "Fu Li" and "Feng Nian", which recorded and sang the praises of a happy and beautiful time.

However, the years were not kind to him, and after his defeat to Yellow Emperor, the aged Emperor Yan became discouraged and retreated to the south, no longer having the courage to compete with Yellow Emperor for supremacy. Xingtian's loyalty to Emperor Yan was so great that he repeatedly begged Emperor Yan to unite with Chiyou and take over the world, but the emperor took

alliance
n. 联盟

no action. When the news came that Chiyou had been defeated and killed in battle, Xing tian's anger spiralled out of control. With a shield in his left hand and a battle-ax in his right, he went alone to the central court of Yellow Emperor, and with an **overwhelming** force, he went straight to the gate of the emperor's palace, naming to fight with the emperor in single combat.

overwhelming
adj. 巨大的

The emperor was furious and took the fight personally. And so, a battle to the death ensued. The two fought from the palace to the outskirts of the city, and then to Mount Changyang where Emperor Yan was born, but the winner or loser couldn't be distinguished yet. Finally, Xingtian lost the battle. The emperor cut off his head and buried it on Mount Changyang. However, Xingtian persevered. After he lost his head, he used his nipples as his eyes and his navel as his mouth and continued to brandish his shield and battle-ax. By doing this, he expressed his fierce spirit that would never submit or give up.

TIPS: Xingtian's heroic and unyielding spirit has attracted and encouraged generations of Chinese people. One of the famous examples is a poem written by Tao Yuanming, a well-known poet in the Eastern Jin Dynasty. The poem "Reading *Shan Hai Jing*" states that "Xingtian brandished his shield and battle-ax, his fierce spirit will live forever."

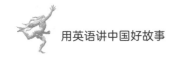

百鸟朝凤

少昊是中国神话五方天帝中的西方天帝,又称白帝,华夏东夷部落的首领。相传少昊是"天降帝王",他的父亲是太白金星,母亲是天宫里的仙女皇娥。

一天,少女皇娥乘着木筏沿着银河玩耍,无意中来到了西海之滨,发现这里有一棵神奇的穷桑树,上千只鸟儿正聚集在这里举行盛会。

"难道这里是鸟的王国?"皇娥正暗自惊讶时,却见从穷桑树上走下来一位少年。这位英俊少年就是看守穷桑树的太白金星,两人一见钟情。

太白金星告诉皇娥:这棵穷桑树要千年一开花,再千年一结果。所结之果若是凡人吃了,能长生不老;若神仙吃了,也会永葆青春。皇娥今天到来时,恰逢穷桑树开始结果的前一天,感召了上千只鸟儿前来聚会。能目睹上千年一次的鸟类节日盛会,是太有缘分了!

据说鸟儿们在此大会上将推选新一届鸟王,也会重新制定鸟类新的规则。

太白金星诚邀皇娥一起参加鸟儿们的节日。他们在穷桑树下一起弹琴、唱歌、跳舞,直到三天后盛会结束。新一届被推选为王的那只凤鸟,离开前与太白金星来了一场"人鸟"对话,鸟王代表鸟类祝福他们俩,希望他们相爱下去。两位年轻人相会穷桑树下,他们爱情的结晶就是少昊。

【阅读小贴士】少昊的出生带着一丝不平凡的鸟神话色彩,也预示着少昊将有不平凡的人生。值得注意的是,太白金星从鸟树走出,故事里选出的新王是一只凤鸟,少昊被称为"百鸟之王",名鸷,也是一只鸷鸟。这些不仅反映当时可能处于母系氏族社会,而且开启了华夏民族"凤文化"之先河。

All Birds Paying Homage to the Phoenix

Shaohao is the Western Heavenly Emperor of the five emperors of Chinese mythology, also known as the White Emperor, and the leader of the Eastern Yi tribe in China. According to Chinese legends, he was the "emperor descending from the sky", his father was the God Venus and his mother was Huang'e, a fairy in the heavenly palace.

One day, while playing along the Milky Way on a raft, the young girl Huang'e accidentally came to the shore of the Western Sea and found a magical **mulberry tree**, where thousands of birds were gathering for a festival.

"Could this place be the kingdom of the birds?" Huang'e was secretly surprised when she saw a young boy coming down from the tree. This handsome young man was the God Venus, the guardian of the huge mulberry tree, and they fell in love at first sight.

The young man told her that this tree would blossom once every thousand years and bear fruit once every thousand years. If a mortal ate the fruit, he would live forever; if an immortal ate it, he would also stay young forever. When she arrived today, it was the day before the tree began to bear fruit, and thousands of birds were summoned to the gathering. It was so fortunate to witness

mulberry tree
桑树

the once-in-a-thousand-year bird festival!

It was said that the birds would elect a new king at this assembly and also rewrote the new rules for birds.

The God Venus invited Huang'e to take part in the birds' festival. They played the lute, sang and danced together under the tree until the event ended three days later. Before leaving, the phoenix, who had been elected king for the new term, had a "human-bird" conversation with the God Venus. On behalf of the birds, the bird king wished them both well and hoped that they would continue to love each other. Two young people met under a poor mulberry tree, and their son Shaohao was the fruit of their love.

TIPS: The birth of Shaohao has a touch of extraordinary bird mythology, which also foretells that he will have an extraordinary life. It is noteworthy that the God Venus emerged from the bird tree, that the new king chosen in the story is a phoenix, and that Shaohao is known as "the King of Hundred Birds", named Zhi, also a bird of prey. These not only reflect the **matrilineal** clan society that may have existed at the time but also initiated the "phoenix culture" of the Chinese nation.

matrilineal
adj. 母系的

百鸟国之王少昊

为了儿子少昊将来能承担大任,太白金星和皇娥都不约而同地想到:让少昊到人间去历练。

这一天,黄帝和妻子嫘祖的长子出生时,天空飞来五只美丽的凤凰,落在家中的院子里。这出生的孩子正是少昊。少昊在人间父亲黄帝和母亲嫘祖精心养育下,具有超凡的本领。

少年时,黄帝送少昊到凤鸿氏部落里去历练(东夷部落联盟里的一个最大部落),娶凤鸿氏之女为妻,成为凤鸿部落的首领,以玄鸟(即燕子)作为本部落的图腾。后来,他在东海之滨建立了自己的部落,成为整个东夷部落的首领。当他登上大联盟首领之位时,有凤鸟飞来,少昊见了非常喜欢,于是改以凤鸟为族神,崇拜凤鸟图腾。

少昊建立了一个以凤鸟为图腾的完整的氏族部落社会。所辖部族均以鸟为名,有鸿鸟氏、凤鸟氏、玄鸟氏、青鸟氏等二十四个氏族,而且他的部下臣僚全是以鸟类划分官职,具体分工则是根据不同鸟类的特点来进行。他让凤凰成为总管,百鸟都由他来规范管理。他根据一年四季的不同,安排燕子掌管春天、伯劳掌管夏天、鹦雀掌管秋天、锦鸡掌管冬天。除此之外,他又派了五种鸟来管理日常事务。孝顺的鹁鸪掌管教育,凶猛的鸷鸟掌管军事,公平的布谷掌管建筑,威严的雄鹰掌管法律,善辩的斑鸠掌管言论。另外有九种扈鸟掌管农业,五种野鸡分别掌管木工、漆工、陶工、染工、皮工五个工种。

少昊成了一位真正的鸟国之王,他针对鸟儿们的生活习性为鸟们建立了一整套管理体系,每到开朝会时,少昊便坐在朝堂中间,倾听百鸟争鸣。他天生听得懂鸟语,赏罚分明,公平公正,让每一类鸟都找到自己的位置,发挥自己的才能。少昊编制出了一套完善的鸟类官位体系,成为统领一方

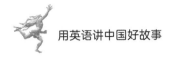

的明君。

【阅读小贴士】少昊神仙下凡的身世背景，反映了后人对历史上少昊具有的才能和功绩的崇拜，进而神化。相传少昊在位时间长达八十四年，编制出了一套完善的鸟国官位体系，在部落诞生了凤文化。到春秋战国时期，华夏凤文化和龙文化合并交融成龙凤文化，成为华夏民族两大文化支柱。

Shaohao, King of Birds

In order for their son Shaohao to take on great responsibilities in the future, both the God Venus and Huang'e had the **unanimous** idea to let him go to earth for experience.

On this day, when Yellow Emperor and his wife Lei Zu's eldest son was born, five beautiful phoenixes flew from the sky and landed in the courtyard of their home. The child born was none other than Shaohao. He was carefully nurtured by his parents and was endowed with extraordinary skills.

As a teenager, Shaohao was sent by Yellow Emperor to the Feng Hong tribe (one of the largest tribes in the Eastern Yi tribal alliance) for training. He married the daughter of the tribe, became the leader and took the Xuan bird (swallow) as the totem of the tribe. Later, he founded his own tribe on the shores of the East China Sea and became the chief of the entire Eastern Yi tribes. When he ascended to the position of chief of the Grand Alliance, a phoenix flew in and he was so fond of seeing it that he changed to the phoenix as his clan god and worshiped the phoenix totem.

He established a complete clan and tribal society with the phoenix as its totem. The clans under his **jurisdiction**

unanimous

adj. 一致的

jurisdiction

n. 管辖权

were all named after birds, and there were twenty-four clans, including the Hong Bird Clan, the Feng Bird Clan, the Xuan Bird Clan and the Qing Bird Clan. Moreover, his ministers were all divided into official positions according to birds, and the specific division of labour was based on the characteristics of different birds. He allowed the phoenix to become the chief governor, and all the birds were regulated by him. According to the differences of four seasons in a year, he assigned the swallow to be in charge of the spring, the shrike to be in charge of the summer, the parrot to be in charge of the autumn and the golden pheasant to be in charge of the winter. In addition, he assigned five other birds to manage the daily affairs. The **filial** wood pigeon was in charge of education, the fierce bird of prey was in charge of military, the fair bungee was in charge of construction, the majestic eagle was in charge of law, and the eloquent turtle dove was in charge of speech. There were also other nine species of birds of prey in charge of agriculture, and five species of pheasants in charge of five crafts: carpenters, **lacquerers**, potters, dyers and leather workers.

He became a true king of the bird kingdom, and he set up a whole system of management for the birds according to their habits. At every court meeting, he sat in the middle of the court and listened to the voices of birds. He was born to understand the language of the birds, and he rewarded and punished them in a fair and just manner, so that each type of bird could find its own place and give full

filial
adj. 孝顺的

lacquerer
n. 漆匠

play to its talents. He compiled a perfect system of official positions for birds and became a wise ruler who ruled over one side.

TIPS: The background of Shaohao's divine descent into the world reflects the worship and deification of the talents and achievements he possessed in history by later generations. According to legend, his reign lasted 84 years, compiling a perfect system of official positions in the bird kingdom and giving birth to the phoenix culture in the tribe. By the Spring and Autumn Period and Warring States Period, the Chinese phoenix culture and dragon culture merged and mingled to form the dragon and phoenix culture, which become the two cultural pillars of the Chinese nation.

管理家仓颉

传说仓颉是中国汉字的首创人，他的特别之处是生有"双瞳"。一双眼睛总是炯炯有神，深得轩辕黄帝赏识，收在身边当个史官。

黄帝分派他专门管理圈里牲口、屯里食物的增减，类似于现在的仓库保管员。不过那个年代没有文字可以记录，全靠仓颉过人的记忆本领。

在工作中，仓颉逐渐积累了一些经验。譬如，在存放牲口和食物的地方，用绳子打结来代表数目。每当减少数目时，就去解开相同数目的结。为提高效率，仓颉又加以改进，用绳子打圈圈，在圈子里放入贝壳、树枝、石块等来代表他所管的不同东西。增加数目就添一个，减少就去掉一个，这法子挺管用，再也不用打结、解结那么麻烦了。

黄帝见仓颉聪明能干，就把每年祭祀的次数、狩猎的分配、部落人丁的增减统统交给仓颉去管。时间长了，管的事情多了，仓颉也难免记错。他曾经就出过一件大错，把谈判用的物资数据搞错了，导致黄帝和炎帝的谈判失败。此后仓颉一直自责、惭愧，工作更加辛苦了。

一天，仓颉参加集体狩猎，走到一个三岔路口时，几位老人为走哪条路争辩起来。有说要往东走，说有野猪；有说要往北走，说可以追到鹿群；还有偏要往西，说有两只老虎，不及时打死，就会错过了机会。仓颉一问，原来他们是看地上野兽的脚印才认定的。仓颉心中猛然一喜：既然不同的脚印代表不同野兽，是不是可以用不同的符号来表示我所管的东西呢？他回到家，开始苦思冥想起来，在地上画出各种符号来表示事物。果然，把事情管理得头头是道。

黄帝知道后，大加赞赏，命令仓颉到各个部落去传授这种管理方法。

【阅读小贴士】在仓颉造字以前，人们以结绳来记事，即大事打一大结，小事打一小结，相连的事打一连环结。后又发展到用刀子在木竹上刻以符号作为记事，当结绳和刻木的方法都不能适应需要时，仓颉从实践中总结出用不同符号来加强有效管理的办法，与文字的创造越来越近了。

Cangjie Specializing in Management

According to legend, Cangjie was the first creator of Chinese characters, and his special feature was that he had "double pupils". His eyes were always shining, and he was so **appreciated** by Yellow Emperor Xuanyuan that he took him on as a historian.

appreciate
v. 赏识

He was assigned by Yellow Emperor to manage the increase and decrease of livestock in the pens and food in the tunnels, similar to a warehouse keeper nowadays. In those days, however, there was no written record, so it was all down to his excellent memory skills.

In the course of the work, he gradually gained some experience. For example, in the area where the livestock and food were kept, a **knotted string** was used to represent the number. Whenever the number was reduced, the same number of knots would be untied. To improve the efficiency, he improved it by tying loops of rope and putting shells, branches and stones in the loops to represent the different things under his control. If the number increased, one would be added, and if it decreased, one would be removed. This method worked well, and it was no longer necessary to untie the knots.

knotted string
结绳

Seeing that Cangjie was smart and capable, Yellow Emperor gave him the task of managing the number of

annual rituals, the distribution of hunting and the increase and decrease of tribal population. As time went on, he had to take care of more things and inevitably made mistakes. There was a big mistake once, when he made a mistake in the data of the materials used for **negotiation**, which led to the failure of the negotiation between Yellow Emperor and Emperor Yan. After that, he blamed himself and was ashamed, and worked even harder.

negotiation
n. 谈判；协商

One day, when he was on a group hunt, he came to a three-way intersection and several old men argued over which way to go. Some said they wanted to go east, saying there were wild boars; some said they wanted to go north, saying they could chase the deer; others preferred to go west, saying there were two tigers and if they did not kill them in time, they would miss their chance. When he asked, it turned out that they had determined by looking at the footprints of the beasts on the ground. His heart **snapped with** joy: Since different footprints represent different beasts, can I use different symbols to indicate what I am in charge of? He returned home and began to contemplate, drawing various symbols on the ground to represent things. Certainly, he managed things in order.

snap with
咬住

When the emperor learned of it, he appreciated it and ordered him to go to various tribes to teach this management method.

TIPS: Before Cangjie invented the characters, people used knotted ropes to keep track of things, i.e. a big knot for big things, a small knot for small things, and a chain of knots for connected things. Then they used a knife to carve symbols into wood and bamboo as a notation. When both the knotted rope and the carved wood methods failed to meet the needs, Cangjie concluded from practice that different symbols could be used to enhance effective management, getting closer and closer to the invention of characters.

仓颉造字

仓颉创造的"符号管理法",得到黄帝的支持,并要求仓颉到各个部落去推广这种记事方法。

在推广使用过程中,一位老人对仓颉提出疑问:有些符号不易理解,不易理解就影响记忆。仓颉觉得有理,此后每造一个符号,总要反复推敲,广泛征求意见,大家都说"好"时,才定下来,分享到各个部落,并及时修改完善发现的问题。

仓颉开始有意识地用符号来代替万物,认真研究每一种符号表达的意思。一天,仓颉随轩辕黄帝南巡,看到水边有人捕到一只大龟,龟背上面有许多青色花纹。仓颉被吸引了,便取来细细观察,发现龟背上的花纹竟是有意义可循的。他想花纹既能表意,如果定下一个规则,岂不是人人都可用来传达心意,记载事情了?

仓颉晚上做了一个神奇的梦,梦见那只大龟在对着他微笑。他从梦中惊醒,忽然开窍,灵感大发,随即研究野兽的脚印,在石崖上描摹刻下二十八个兽蹄鸟迹的符号,成为最早的"汉字"。

仓颉自受神龟背上青色花纹点悟之后,心中豁然开朗,从此细心观察研究世间万物。他从天上星宿的分布情况,到地上山川脉络的样子,再到鸟兽虫鱼的痕迹、草木器具的形状,都去不停地描摹绘写,造出种种不同的符号,并且确定每种符号所代表的意义。等他按自己的心意,用符号拼凑成几段来表达意义后,便拿去给别人看,经他解说后,别人也能看得明白。仓颉把这些符号叫做"字"。

【阅读小贴士】实践出真知。仓颉在观察自然万象中不断总结、创新，创造出中国最原始的象形文字，从而结束了远古时期结绳记事的蒙昧时代，被后人尊称为"造字圣人"。其实，汉字的诞生非一人一手之功，应该是先民长期累积发展的结果。流传下来的仓颉造字的传说，说明仓颉是在汉字发展中具有特别重大贡献的人物，他可能是整理汉字的集大成者。如今"仓颉造字传说"已列入非遗名录，代表中华民族对人类文明的巨大贡献。

 神话故事

Cangjie Inventing Chinese Characters

Cangjie's invention of the "symbolic management method" was supported by Yellow Emperor, who asked him to go to all tribes to **promote** this method of note-making.

promote
v. 推进；促进

In the process of promoting the use of symbols, an old man questioned him: some symbols were not easy to understand, and if they were difficult to understand, they would affect memory. He felt that this thought was a valid point, and from then on, every time he created a symbol, he had to weigh it repeatedly and **solicit** opinions widely, and only when everyone said it was "good" did he finalize it and share it with the tribes, and promptly amend it to improve any problems he found.

solicit
v. 索求；征求

He began to **consciously** use symbols to replace all things, carefully studying the meaning of each symbol. One day, he was on a southern tour with Yellow Emperor, seeing a large turtle caught by someone at the water's edge, with many green patterns on its back. He was intrigued, took it and looked at it carefully, and found that the patterns on the turtle's back had a meaning to follow. He thought that since the patterns could be used to express ideas, if a rule was laid down, would it be possible for everyone to use them to convey their thoughts and record

consciously
adv. 有意识地

101

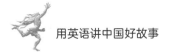

things?

At night, he had a magical dream in which he saw the turtle smiling at him. He woke up from his dream, suddenly **enlightened** and inspired, and then studied the footprints of the beast, traced and carved twenty-eight symbols of animal hooves and bird tracks on the stone cliff, which became the earliest "Chinese characters".

enlighten

v. 启发；阐明

After being enlightened by the navy blue patterns on the back of the turtle, he began to carefully observe and study all things in the world. From the distribution of the stars in the sky, to the appearance of the mountains and rivers on the earth, to the traces of birds, animals, insects and fish, to the shapes of grass and wood utensils, he traced and drew them all, creating different symbols and determining the meaning of each. After he had pieced together the symbols to express the meaning as he wished, he showed them to others, who could then understand them after his explanation. He called these symbols "characters".

TIPS: Practice makes true knowledge. Cangjie continued to summarize and **innovate** in observing all natural phenomena, and invented the most primitive Chinese pictographs, thus ending the obscure era of the ancient period of knotted rope notation, and was revered by later generations as the Sage of Character Invention. In fact, the birth of Chinese characters was not the work of one person, but would have been the result of a long-term cumulative development by the ancestors. The legend of Cangjie inventing characters,

innovate

v. 创新；改革

which has been handed down to us, suggests that he was a particularly significant contributor to the development of Chinese characters, and that he may have been the representative who collated the characters. The legend of his invention of characters is now included in the list of non-traditional heritage, representing the great contribution of the Chinese nation to human civilization.

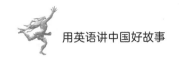

夸父追日

相传在黄帝时代，北方巨人族有一个部落首领叫夸父。为让部落生存下去，夸父决心解决北方常年寒冷的问题。他向族人宣布，他要把太阳"捉"回来，让它永久地挂在天空上，给人们享受阳光和温暖。

第二天，天刚亮，夸父就踏上追赶太阳的征途，发誓不捉回太阳，决不回头。

太阳从东海升起，他就飞向东方，迎着太阳而上。当他发现太阳就在自己头顶上方时，就奋力跃起去摘，结果发现天空远比他想象的要高远得多，他根本就摘不着太阳。

怎么办？眼看太阳向西方而去，他飞奔到一座高山上，想等太阳经过时，能站在山顶上捉住它。可是，他再次失望了。当他站在最高的山顶上，哪怕举起手杖，还是差那么一截。夸父急了，对着太阳大喊："太阳，太阳，请你停下来吧……"太阳仿佛听见他的喊声，逃得更快了。

夸父没有绝望。他认为太阳每天落山的山谷一定离地面最近。于是，夸父狂奔九天九夜，终于赶在太阳落山时刻到达山谷。一团大火球就在夸父身边燃烧着，他伸手就要去摘，太阳的炎热烤得他嗓子直冒烟，仿佛整个身体都要被烤干了。"不能就此倒下！"夸父这样提醒自己，然后他去找水喝。他一口气喝干了黄河和渭河的水，又去北方喝大湖里的水，可惜还没有到达湖边，就因为又累又渴，倒在地上，再也没有起来。他的身躯化作了夸父山，他扔出去的手杖化成桃林，从此夸父山下的这片桃林，不仅为来往这里的过客遮阴避暑，还结出的鲜桃，为过客解渴。

【阅读小贴士】夸父追日是为了给人类采撷火种，使大地获得光明与温暖，故夸父有"盗火英雄"之称，是中国的普罗米修斯。作为神话典故，"夸父追日"有不同寓意，褒义为比喻有宏大志向，也比喻人类战胜自然的决心和雄心壮志；贬义为自不量力。

Kuafu Chasing the Sun

According to legend, during the time of Yellow Emperor, the northern Giants had a tribal leader called Kuafu. In order for the tribe to survive, the leader was determined to solve the problem of the **perennial** cold in the north. He announced to his tribe that he would "catch" the sun back and let it hang in the sky **permanently** to give people sunshine and warmth.

The next day, just after dawn, he set out on his quest to chase the sun, vowing never to turn back until he had caught it.

As the sun rose from the East China Sea, he flew to the east and reached for it. When he found that the sun was just above his head, he leapt up to pick it, only to find that the sky was much higher and farther away than he had imagined, and he could not pick it at all.

What to do? Seeing that the sun was heading west, he raced to a high mountain, hoping to catch it on the top of the mountain when it passed by. But he was disappointed again. When he stood on the top of the highest mountain, even with his cane raised, he was still at a distance from the sun. He was desperate and shouted to the sun, "Sun, sun, please stop..." As if hearing his shout, the sun fled even faster.

perennial
adj. 长久的；持续的
permanently
adv. 永久地；一直

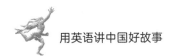

He did not despair. He thought that the valley where the sun sets every day must be closest to the ground. So he ran wildly for nine days and nine nights, and finally reached the valley at the moment of sunset. A big ball of fire was burning right next to him and he reached out to pluck it. The heat of the sun baked his throat straight to smoke, as if his whole body was drying up. "I can't go down at this moment!" He reminded himself and then he went to look for water to drink. He drained the water of the Yellow River and Wei River in one **gulp**, and then went north to drink water from the great lake. Unfortunately, before he reached the lake, he fell to the ground because he was tired and thirsty, and never got up again. His body was transformed into Mount Kuafu, and the walking stick he threw out was transformed into a peach forest. Since then, this peach forest under the mountain not only provided shade for the passers-by who come and go here, but also produced fresh peaches to **quench** their thirst.

TIPS: The purpose of Kuafu's sun-chasing is to gather fire for mankind, so that the earth can be bright and warm, so Kuafu is known as the "fire-stealing hero" and is the Chinese Prometheus. As a mythological allusion, "Kuafu Chasing the Sun" has different meanings, including a positive one: it is a metaphor for people who have great ambitions, and for mankind's determination and **ambition** to overcome nature; and a negative one: do something beyond one's ability.

gulp

n. 一大口

quench

v. 解（渴）；止（渴）

ambition

n. 夙愿

帝尧出生

帝尧是中国古代的仁君，帝喾与庆都之子，黄帝的曾孙。

尧的出生充满着传奇色彩。传说尧的母亲庆都有一次在河上游玩，发现有一条赤龙，围绕在小船周围飞来飞去，久久不愿离去，仿佛有什么话要对她诉说。第二天，庆都特意再次来到河上，这次出现了一条形体小些的赤龙。庆都认为"龙"是吉祥之物，预示着有好事发生。

有什么好事发生呢？庆都晚上做了一个梦，梦见自己怀孕了，还有一张画像。十四个月后，庆都生下一个男孩，和画上的人一模一样。这个孩子就是尧。后来帝喾把王位传给了尧的异母兄长挚。帝挚在位九年，自觉才能平庸，没有尧圣明。于是，在尧二十岁时，挚让位给尧。

帝尧在位七十年，行仁政，爱人民，深得民心。

【阅读小贴士】尧的出生有多种说法，但有一种现象更值得注意，就是这里讲到的，尧的父亲属于黄帝部落，母亲属于炎帝部落。要知道，黄帝和炎帝是历史上发生大战的敌人，而尧是他们的后代，至少说明两点：一是体现了部落和民族的和解和融合；二是尧堪称炎黄子孙的典型代表，是中华民族的始祖之一。

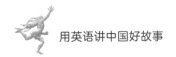

Birth of Emperor Yao

Emperor Yao was a benevolent ruler in ancient China. He was the son of Emperor Ku and Qingdu and the great-grandson of Yellow Emperor.

His birth was full of legends. Legend has it that once on a visit to the river, his mother, Qingdu, noticed a red dragon flying around a small boat, unwilling to leave for a long time, as if the dragon had something to say to her. The next day, she **deliberately** came to the river again, and this time a smaller red dragon appeared. She believed that the "dragon" is an **auspicious** object and that it was a sign of good things to come.

What was the good news? She had a dream at night that she was pregnant and there was a portrait of a man. Fourteen months later, she gave birth to a boy who looked exactly like the man in the painting. This child was Yao. Later, Emperor Ku passed the throne to Yao's elder half-brother, Zhi. Emperor Zhi reigned for nine years, but felt that his talents were **mediocre** and not as wise as those of Yao, so when Yao was twenty years old, Zhi gave up his throne to him.

Emperor Yao **reigned** for seventy years and was a benevolent ruler who loved his people and won their hearts.

deliberately
adv. 故意地

auspicious
adj. 吉祥的

mediocre
adj. 平庸的；平常的

reign
v. 为王；为君

神话故事

TIPS: There are various accounts of Yao's birth, but one more noteworthy phenomenon is that, as mentioned here, Yao's father belonged to Yellow Emperor tribe and his mother belonged to Emperor Yan tribe. It is understood that Yellow Emperor and Yan Emperor were enemies who had great wars throughout history, but Yao is their descendant, which means at least two things: firstly, his birth **embodies** the **reconciliation** and integration of tribes and peoples; and secondly, Yao is a typical representative of the descendant of Emperor Yan and Yellow Emperor, and is one of the earliest ancestors of the Chinese nation.

embody
v. 体现

reconciliation
n. 和解；调解

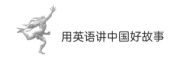

帝尧知人善任

尧即位后,首先重用本族贤者,紧密团结族人,做到"九族既睦";又考察官员的政绩,奖善罚恶,使政务井然有序;同时协调各邦族间的关系,使老百姓和睦相处。

尧善于发现和使用人才,聚集了一大批贤臣,也让人才充分发挥才能。他让弃(后稷,周始祖,也称稷神)做农师,主抓农业;让舜做司徒,主抓教育;让契做司马,主抓军事;让锤做工师,主抓工业,让夔(kuí)做乐官,主抓文化;让皋陶做大理,主抓司法。总之,尧展示出非凡的领袖能力。在尧的治理下,政治清明,世风祥和,天下安宁。

尧还制定了历法,教人们依时按节从事生产活动。《史记·五帝本纪》中记载:"乃命羲、和,敬顺昊天,数法日月星辰,敬授民时。"帝尧命羲氏、和氏掌管天文历法,派羲仲、羲叔、和仲、和叔四人分驻四方,负责观察和记录日月星辰运转,修订历法,制定农时,指导百姓生产耕作。他们根据日出日落的方位和昼夜长短的变化,将天象和物象相对应,确定了春分、夏至、秋分与冬至四个节气,并且以增加闰月的方法将四时节气的轮回与太阳回归周期相对应。

二分、二至确定以后,尧决定以三百六十六日为一年,每三年置一闰月,用闰月调整历法和四季的关系,使每年的农时正确,不出差错。

由此可知,帝尧时代是农耕文化飞跃发展的时代。

【阅读小贴士】"知人善任"不仅是帝尧成就伟业的制胜法宝,也是今天成大事者的基本能力。

Emperor Yao
Making Good Use of Able Persons

After his accession to the throne, Emperor Yao first reused the sages of his own tribe, uniting them closely and ensuring that "the nine tribes were in harmony with each other". He also examined the performance of the officials, rewarded good and punished evil, **distinguished** between the high and low, so that the government was orderly; and coordinated the relations between the various states and tribes so that the common people lived in harmony.

He was good at discovering able people and put them at suitable posts, gathering a large number of wise officials and allowing them to give full play to their talents. He appointed Qi (Houji, Zhou founder; Lord of Millet) as a officer in charge of agriculture, Shun as the Minister for Education, Qi as a chancellor of wars focusing on military affairs, Chui as a worker focusing on industry, Kui as a master of music focusing on culture, and Gaoyao as the Minister for Justice. In short, he demonstrated extraordinary leadership skills. Under his rule, politics was clear, the general mood of society was peaceful and the world was **tranquil**.

He also established the calendar and taught the people to engage in productive activities according to the seasons. In the *Historical Records of the Five Emperors*,

distinguish

v. 区分

tranquil

adj. 平静的；安宁的

it is recorded that "Emperor Yao ordered Xi and He to respect and obey the heaven, to count the sun, moon and stars, and to teach the people the calendar". The emperor appointed Xi and He to be in charge of astronomy and calendars, and assigned four men, Xi Zhong, Xi Shu, He Zhong and He Shu, to **be stationed in** the four directions to observe and record the movements of the sun, moon and stars, revise the calendar, set the agricultural seasons and guide the people in their production and cultivation. They corresponded celestial and physical phenomena and then determined the four seasons, namely spring, summer, autumn and winter, according to the direction of sunrise and sunset and the changes in the length of day and night, and by adding leap months, the cycle of the four seasons corresponded to the solar return cycle.

After the **equinoxes** and **solstices** were determined, he decided that the year should be divided into three hundred and sixty-six days, with a leap month every three years. The leap months were used to adjust the relations between the calendar and the four seasons so that the agricultural time of the year would be correct and no mistakes would be made.

It is clear from this story that the Emperor Yao era was a time when farming culture developed by **leaps and bounds**.

TIPS: "Knowing how to make good use of able persons" is not only the winning formula for Emperor Yao to accomplish great achievements, but also a fundamental ability for those who achieve greatness today.

---

be stationed in
驻扎

equinox
n. 昼夜平分时；（春/秋）分

solstice
n. 至（点）；（夏/冬）至

leaps and bounds
突飞猛进

帝尧禅让

尧以德治国，作风民主，善于纳谏，具有治国安邦的雄才大略。他在位七十年，深得民心。他不以天子之位为私有，传贤不传子，把帝位禅让给舜的故事，成为历史佳话。

尧的长子丹朱，自幼聪明，深受尧的宠爱。但丹朱的兴趣在围棋上，有史上"第一围棋高手"之称，甚至被后人誉为世界围棋始祖。尧尊重儿子的爱好，深知儿子不是帝王最合格的人选。尧帝召开部落联盟议事会议，讨论继承人的人选问题。大家都推荐虞舜，说他是个德才兼备的人。

尧决定先考察一番，再做决定。尧首先大胆决定把自己的两个女儿娥皇、女英同时嫁给舜，从两个女儿那里考察他的德行，看他是否能理好家政；然后又派舜负责推行德教，舜便教导臣民以"五典"——父义、母慈、兄友、弟恭、子孝这五种美德指导自己的言行，臣民都听从教诲，依照"五典"行事。尧又让舜总管百官和处理政务，舜照样处理得有条不紊。尧还让舜负责接待四方前来朝见的诸侯，舜和诸侯之间和睦友好，彼此敬重。最后，尧让舜独自去山麓的森林中经受大自然的考验。舜在暴风雷雨中，没有迷失方向，显示出很强的生存能力。

经过三年多各种各样的考察，尧觉得舜这个人无论说话办事，都很成熟可靠，而且很贤明。于是选择这一年的正月初一，帝尧在太庙举行禅位典礼，让舜正式接替自己。尧退位后二十八年去世，百姓像失去自己的父母那样悲哀，三年之间，自觉不举办任何娱乐活动，以表达对尧的爱戴和哀思。

【阅读小贴士】尧废除首领世袭制，以天下苍生为重，任人唯贤，让贤于舜，特别是亲自设置各害考题，考察推荐人选，体现了尧的英明、智慧、民主和务实；开创了国家治理新模式，其高尚的政德是后人为官从政的学习榜样。

Emperor Yao Ceding the Throne

Emperor Yao ruled the country with virtue, was democratic in his manner and was good at accepting advice, and had the eloquence to rule the country and secure the state. He reigned for seventy years and won the respect of the people. He did not take the throne of the emperor as private, passed it to sages rather than sons, and handed over the crown to Shun, which became a historical story.

His eldest son, Danzhu, was intelligent from an early age and was much loved by his father. But his interest was in *weiqi*(Go), he was known as "the First Go Master" in history, and was even hailed by later generations as the originator of Go in the world. He respected his son's hobby and knew that he was not the most qualified candidate for the position of emperor. He convened a tribal alliance council to discuss the choice of a successor. Everyone recommended Yu Shun, saying that he was a man of both virtue and talent.

He decided to examine him first before making a decision. He first **boldly** decided to marry his two daughters Ehuang and Nüying to Shun at the same time, in order to observe his virtue and see if he could manage the household well. Shun was then put in charge of moral

boldly
adv. 大胆的

education, and he taught his subjects to use the "Five Classics" —righteousness of father, kindness of mother, friendship of brother, respect of younger brother, and filial piety of son to guide their words and actions. The subjects followed the teachings and acted in accordance with the "Five Classics". The emperor put Shun in charge of all the officials and government affairs, and Shun handled them in an orderly manner. He also put Shun in charge of the reception of lords who came from all directions to see him, Shun and the lords were friendly and respectful of each other. Finally, he sent Shun to the forest at the foot of the mountain to be tested by nature alone. Shun did not lose his way in the storm and thunderstorm and showed great ability to survive.

After more than three years of various examinations, he felt that Shun was a mature and reliable person in both speech and deeds, and was very wise. So on the first day of the first month of that year, he chose to hold a meditation ceremony at the Imperial Temple, allowing Shun to formally succeed himself. When he died twenty-eight years after his **abdication**, the people mourned as if their own parents died and they consciously **refrained** from holding any entertainment between three years to show their love and mourning for him.

TIPS: Emperor Yao abolished the **hereditary** system of chiefs, put the lives of the people first, appointed people on their merit, and ceded the crown to Shun. In particular,

abdication
n. 禅让

refrain
v. 克制；节制

hereditary
adj. 世袭的

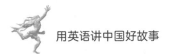

he personally set tests in various areas to inspect the recommended candidates, reflecting his wisdom, intelligence, democracy and **pragmatism**. He created a new model of national governance, and his noble political virtues are an example for future generations to follow in their careers in politics.

pragmatism
n. 实用主义

神话故事

帝尧嫁女

"尧之二女，舜之二妃"，这是历史上帝尧嫁女的佳话。帝尧将两个宝贝女儿同时嫁给同一人，这人就是经帝尧多次考验，并最终禅让王位的舜，这体现出帝尧的智慧、勇敢和牺牲精神。

女儿们相信父王的安排，可女儿们的母亲为难了。原来大女儿娥皇是养女，小女儿女英才是她与尧亲生的，平时对姐妹二人平等相待，但姐妹同嫁一人，就有正室和偏房之分，怎么安排，都会觉得对不起其中一个女儿。

尧出了三道考题，让女儿们比赛，以比赛结果解决难题。

考题一：煮豆子。给两个女儿各十粒豆子，五斤柴火，先煮熟者胜。娥皇从小协助做饭，有经验，只往锅内倒了适量水，柴没用完，豆子就煮熟了。女英却相反，水放太多，柴烧完了水还没烧沸。

考题二：纳鞋底。分给两个女儿各一只鞋底和一把纳绳子，谁先纳成谁胜。姐姐娥皇把长绳剪成短节，纳完一根，再接上一根纳。一只鞋底不到半天工夫就纳成了，还纳得平展好看。而女英这边呢，一根长绳总打结，半天下来，半只鞋底都没有纳好，针脚还歪歪扭扭，稀而不平。

女儿出嫁动身前，尧出了第三道考题：谁先到历山下舜的住地者为胜。这时尧妻说：坐马车有排场，应让给姐姐娥皇坐。让亲生女儿单人骑走骡。尧明知妻子偏心，也不愿意点破，想到娥皇已胜了两局，也就随她去了。

按说这次女英必赢无疑，可恰巧女英所骑走骡有孕在身，跑急了，动了胎气，突然就下驹不能走了。女英见离舜的居地已经太远，只好跑步前行，快到时却跑不动了，在路边歇下喘气。这时，娥皇的马车也赶到了，娥皇见妹妹累成这样，立即下车把妹妹拉上马车，一同出发。

舜和娥皇、女英两姐妹成亲后，对她们百般疼爱，没有偏正之分。姐妹俩齐心协力辅佐舜治理天下，也被天下人爱戴。

【阅读小贴士】帝尧将两个女儿同时嫁给舜,并不是因为自己要传位于舜,看重舜的未来前途,而是想通过两个女儿考察舜的品德和能力。这有很大的风险,如果舜不是正人君子,那后果不堪设想;但同时也体现帝尧对舜有信心,才敢把两个女儿都嫁给舜。这是怎样的一位父亲啊!

Emperor Yao Marrying His Daughters

"Yao's two daughters, Shun's two concubines", this is a much-told tale in history about the marriage of Emperor Yao's daughters. The emperor married his two precious daughters to the same person at the same time. This person was Shun, who was tested many times by the Emperor Yao and eventually abdicated the throne, reflecting the emperor's wisdom, bravery and spirit of sacrifice.

The daughters trusted their father's arrangement, but the daughters' mother was in a dilemma. It turned out that the eldest daughter, Ehuang, was an adopted daughter and the youngest daughter, Nüying, was her own child with Yao. Usually the two sisters were treated equally, but when they married the same person, there was a distinction between the offical wife and the **concubine**, and no matter how she were arranged, she would feel sorry for one of the daughters.

Yao came up with three exam questions and asked the daughters to compete to solve the problems with the results of the competition.

Exam question one: cooking beans. The two daughters were given ten beans and five pounds of firewood each, and the first one to make the beans cooked won. Ehuang

concubine

n. 妾；偏房

grew up helping to cook, so she had experience. She only poured the right amount of water into the pot, firewood was not used up, the beans were cooked. On the contrary, Nüying put too much water, when the firewood finished burning, the water had not yet boiled.

Exam question two: Making the soles of shoes. The two daughters were given a sole and a handful of string each, and the one who finished first won. The older sister cut the long rope into short sections, finished one and then picked up another. It took less than half a day to finish one shoe sole, and it was even flattened out beautifully. Take a look at Nüying's approach: the long rope was always knotted, and half a day later, half the sole was not even finished, and the stitches were **crooked** and uneven.

crooked
adj. 弯曲的

Before his daughter left for her wedding, Yao asked a third question: whoever reached Shun's place at the bottom of Mount Li first would be the winner. At this point his wife said, "A carriage ride is a bit of a show, so I should give it to the elder sister Ehuang and let our own daughter ride the mule alone." He knew that his wife was biased, but he was reluctant to point it out to her, thinking that Ehuang had already won two games, he agreed with his wife's idea.

It should have been a sure win for Nüying this time. But it so happened that the mule she was riding was pregnant, and when she ran fast, it got sick and suddenly couldn't go. When she saw that she was too far from Shun's place, she had to run. Nearing the destination, she

couldn't run anymore and rested on the side of the road to catch her breath. At that moment, Ehuang's carriage arrived. Seeing that her sister was so tired, she immediately got out of the carriage, pulled her into the carriage and set off together.

After the marriage of Shun and the two sisters, he treated them with love and affection and did not **discriminate** between them. The two sisters worked together to help their husband rule the world and were loved by all the people in the world.

discriminate

v. 区别；辨别

TIPS: The reason why Emperor Yao married his two daughters to Shun at the same time was not because he wanted to cede the crown to Shun, but because he wanted to examine Shun's morality and ability through his two daughters, which was a great risk. If Shun had not been a decent man, the consequences would have been unthinkable. But at the same time it also showed that the emperor had faith in Shun before he dared to marry both his daughters to him. What a father he was!

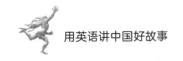

羿射九日

远古时候，大地出现了严重的旱灾，炎热烤焦了森林，烘干了大地，晒干了禾苗草木。原来，帝俊和妻子羲和生了十个孩子都是太阳。他们像一只只熊熊燃烧的火鸟，照耀着大地。母亲羲和陪伴着他们居住在东海中的岛上。他们常在东海里洗澡，然后像鸟儿那样栖息在岛中的一棵叫扶桑的参天大树上。他们的使命是每天委派一个太阳兄弟从东海升入天空去执勤，给大地万物带去光明和温暖。

这样年复一年，十个兄弟每天轮换着升入天空，让人们日出而耕，日落而息。一天，有个兄弟抱怨这样的日子太单调了。他的话引起九个兄弟的共鸣，于是趁母亲生病离开的晚上，十兄弟密议一起任性一次。第二天，可怕的事情发生了，十个太阳同时升上了天空，顿时让大地上所有的生命都像热锅上的蚂蚁，惶惶不可终日。而天空中的十兄弟却释放着天性，玩得开心。此后他们乐此不疲，连着好多天一起升空玩耍，一点也没有想到，大地万物因为它们如此任性都快被烤焦了。

帝尧命羿射十日，羿射下了天上的九个太阳。

羿跋山涉水，去寻找太阳，一路上目睹十个太阳带给人间的灾难，气愤不已。在十兄弟刚刚爬上天空时，就劝他们退回去九个。可太阳兄弟十分傲慢，自以为是帝俊之子，仍然我行我素。羿苦口婆心地劝了一天，以为第二天会有所改变。没想到第二天一早，十个太阳又一起无所顾忌地升空了，羿再次警告无果，忍无可忍，直接拉弓射箭，只听"嗖嗖"几声，九个火辣辣的太阳掉落了，唯一活下的太阳吓得躲进了大海里，瞬间世界变得一片黑暗。

最后天帝出面，唤回了躲在海里的太阳，从此他乖乖地履职尽责，成为人类万物的好朋友。

【阅读小贴士】羿射九日这个神话故事很有教育意义。帝俊的九个儿子如果能接受劝诫，多些怜悯心，不仗势欺人，也不至于乐极生悲，丢了性命。

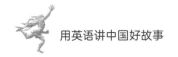

Yi Shooting the Suns

In ancient times, there was a severe drought on the land, and the heat **scorched** the forests, dried up the earth, the grasses and plants. It turned out that Emperor Jun and his wife Xihe had ten children who were all suns. They resembled blazing firebirds, shining on the land. Their mother accompanied them to live on an island in the East China Sea. They often bathed in the East China Sea. Then they perched on a gnarled tree called Fusang like birds. Their mission was to assign one of the brothers to rise from the East China Sea into the sky every day to go on duty and bring light and warmth to all the creatures of the earth.

Year after year, the ten brothers took duty one by one in order, so that the people could plough at sunrise and rest at sunset. However, one day, one of the brothers complained that the days were too **monotonous**. His words **resonated with** the other nine brothers, so they took advantage of their mother's sickness to leave for the night and secretly agreed to rise up together for once. The next day, something terrible happened. Ten suns rose in the sky at the same time, and at once all life on the earth was like ants on a hot pan and caught in a panic. But the ten brothers in the sky unleashed their nature and had a great

scorch
v. 烤焦

monotonous
adj. 单调乏味的

resonate with
引起共鸣

deal of fun. Thereafter they were so happy that they rose up to play together for many days in a row, not thinking for a moment that everything on the earth was about to be scorched because of their **caprice**.

caprice

n. 任性

Then Emperor Yao ordered the hero Yi to shoot down the ten suns in the sky, and Yi shot down nine of them.

Yi **trekked** through the mountains and waded through water to find the suns, and was furious to witness the disasters brought to earth by the ten suns along the way. As soon as the ten brothers climbed into the sky, he advised them to return nine. But they were so arrogant that they thought they were the sons of Emperor Jun and continued to do as they pleased. He spent the day trying to persuade them, thinking that the next day would bring a change. Unexpectedly, the next morning, ten suns rose together again without **scruple**. He warned again to no avail. He could not stand it, so he directly pull the bow and shoot arrows, only to hear "whoosh" a few sounds, and nine hot suns fell. The only living one scared to hide in the sea. The world instantly became dark.

trek

v. 长途跋涉

scruple

n. 顾忌

In the end, the Emperor of Heaven stepped in and called back the sun that was hiding in the sea, and since then he has dutifully performed his duties and become a good friend to all mankind.

TIPS: The mythical story of Yi Shooting the Suns is very educational. If Emperor Jun's nine sons had accepted the **admonition** to be more compassionate and not to bully

admonition

n. 警告，告诫

others with their power, they would not have lost their lives in an overjoyed situation.

神话故事

羿除六害

帝尧之时，天上曾有十个太阳同时出现，导致天气异变，妖魔怪兽恣意横生，到处作乱。六害指的就是肆掠人间的六种凶禽猛兽，帝尧派羿到各地诛灭这六个怪兽。

第一个目标是在中原作恶多端的窫窳。它龙头、虎爪、马蹄、红毛，叫起来像婴儿啼哭，会以此将人骗来吃掉。羿潜入窫窳巢穴，一箭射杀死了窫窳。

第二个怪兽是中原桑林里的一头大野猪封豨。它长有獠牙、铜皮、铁骨，力大无穷。每次出来，见人就撕，毁坏房屋，糟蹋庄稼。羿先用箭射瞎野猪的双眼，然后将它生擒活捉。

诛杀窫窳、捕获封豨之后，羿继续追击南方荒野里的凿齿。它人身兽脸，两根突出嘴外的长牙似凿子，五六尺长，不仅是杀人利器，还用来毁坏房屋、糟蹋庄稼。凿齿听说羿来了，决定趁羿睡觉时突袭他。谁知羿早有准备，一箭射中他的左眼，一箭射中它的后心窝，凿齿嚎叫一声，倒地而死。

第四个怪兽是盘踞洞庭湖的脩蛇，它兴风作浪，掀舟、吃人无数。听说羿来了，脩蛇就潜伏在湖底，销声匿迹。羿寻找多日，历经万难，终在滔天白浪中剑断长蛇。

第五个怪兽是在北方凶水一带为祸百姓的九头怪九婴。它能吐水喷火，在凶水中常掀翻过往船只；见人畜便吃，见房屋、庄稼就毁。羿学牛叫引出九婴，九婴先喷水淹羿，谁知羿的身体随水涨而增高；怪兽于是改喷火，羿纵身腾空而起，避开九条火龙。羿随即拔出九支箭，对准怪兽的九个脑袋连连发射。九婴在躲避中，九个脑袋相互缠绕，结果九条性命一条也没留下。

第六怪兽是巨型鸟大风，它在青丘之泽常掀起狂风，毁屋拔树。羿东征青丘泽，用青丝绳系于箭尾，一箭射中闪电一样飞掠的大风。大风尚欲带伤

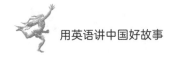

逃生,无奈箭上系绳,只能像一只风筝一样被羿收回。

【阅读小贴士】传说羿五岁时被父母抛弃在深山老林,在野兽口边讨活路,练就了百步穿杨的本领,后来成为帝尧的射师。羿除六害的故事,塑造了一个有勇有谋、一身正气的英雄形象。

Yi Eliminating Six Monsters

At the time of Emperor Yao, there were ten suns in the sky at the same time. This caused a change in the weather, and many ferocious monsters roamed at will and created chaos everywhere. The six monsters were the six kinds of fierce beasts that ravaged the earth. Emperor Yao ordered Yi to wipe out these six monsters in all parts of the world.

The first target was Zhiyu. This monster had done much **mischief** in the central plain. It had a dragon's head, tiger's claws, horse's hooves, red hair and a cry like a baby's. It would use these features to trick people into eating them. Yi **infiltrated** its lair and killed it with a single arrow shot.

The second monster was a large wild boar, Fengxi, in the mulberry forest of the central plain. It had tusks, bronze skin and iron bones, and was extremely powerful. Whenever it came out, it would tear people apart, destroy houses and spoil crops. Yi first blinded the boar with an arrow and then captured it alive.

After killing Zhiyu and capturing Fengxi, he continued to pursue Zaochi in the southern wilderness. It had a human body and a beast's face, with two teeth that protruded from its mouth like **chisels**, five or six feet long, which were not only sharp tools for killing people, but also

mischief
n. 伤害；损害

infiltrate
v. 潜入

chisel
n. 凿子

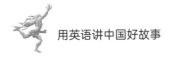

for destroying houses and crops. When the monster heard that Yi was coming, it decided to attack him while he was sleeping. But Yi was prepared and shot it in the left eye and in the back of the heart with arrows. It howled and fell to the ground dead.

The fourth monster was Xiushe(a huge snake). It **coiled** around Dongting Lake, which made waves, lifted boats and ate countless people. When the monster heard that Yi had arrived, it lurked at the bottom of the lake and disappeared. Yi searched for it for many days, and after a lot of difficulties, he finally cut it off with his sword in the overwhelming white waves.

The fifth monster was the nine-head monster Jiuying, which plagued the people around the Xiongshui in the north. It could spit water and breathe fire, and often overturned boats in the water. Whenever it saw animals and people, it ate them, and when it saw houses and crops, it destroyed them. Yi imitated the sound of bull to attract the monster, and the monster firstly sprayed water to drown him, but his body with the water rose and increased in height. It then changed to spew fire, but he rose up in the air, avoiding the nine fire dragons. Then he drew nine arrows and fired them at the nine heads of the monster in quick succession. When the monster tried to avoid the attack, its nine heads wrapped around each other and as a result, none of the nine lives were left behind.

The sixth beast was a giant bird, Dafeng (an enormous bird), which often caused violent winds in rivers along

coil

v. 盘绕

the Qingqiu region, destroying houses and trees. When Yi was on a northern expedition to Qingqiu, he tied a green silk string to the end of his arrow and used it to shot the lighting-fast sweeping monster. It wanted to escape with a wound, but the arrow was tied with a string and was retrieved by Yi like a kite.

TIPS: The story goes that Yi was abandoned by his parents at the age of five in the deep forest. He was able to survive at the mouth of wild beasts and developed the skill of hitting the bull's eye. He later became the archer to Emperor Yao. The story of his eliminating six monsters shapes a heroic figure with courage, resourcefulness and integrity.

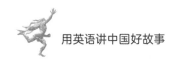

嫦娥奔月

羿为拯救苍生，射下了九个太阳，得罪了天帝，也遭人妒忌。

天帝以百姓需要他除暴安良为由，将他永远贬在人间。羿不能成仙，妻子嫦娥也得跟着丈夫在人间吃苦受累，将来和凡人一样老死。这让羿非常愧疚，觉得对不住妻子。

一天，羿发现嫦娥头上添了白发，更加自责。想起西方昆仑山上的西王母藏有不死之药，就闯过七七四十九关，九死一生，在西王母那里求得不死之药。西王母告诉他，吃了此药可保他与妻子长生不老，如果一个人吃了还可以升天成仙。羿谢别西王母，把仙药交给妻子嫦娥保管，约定第二天八月十五祭拜祖先后，再一起吃下仙药。可万万没有想到，他与妻子的谈话，被心怀不轨的恶徒逢蒙偷听了。

第二天，羿要带弟子们出去练箭，逢蒙便借生病为由留下，逼迫嫦娥交出仙药。嫦娥装作不知，逢蒙却说出自己偷听的事，要强行搜身。眼看着仙药就要被恶徒抢走，嫦娥迫不得已将仙药吞下，顿时觉得自己飞了起来。她舍不得羿，向月亮飞去，一个人寂寞地生活在月宫里，渴望有朝一日能与丈夫团圆。

【阅读小贴士】嫦娥奔月源自古人对星辰的崇拜，据现存文字记载最早出现于《淮南子》等古书。2004年，中国正式开展月球探测工程，并命名为"嫦娥工程"，绕月人造卫星，也以"嫦娥"命名，如"嫦娥一号""嫦娥二号"等。

Chang'e Flying to the Moon

Yi shot down nine surplus suns in order to save the world, offending the Emperor of Heaven and making people jealous.

The emperor relegated him to earth forever on the grounds that the people wanted him to eliminate violence. Yi could not become an immortal and his wife Chang'e had to follow her husband to suffer the hardships on the earth and die like a mortal in the future. This made Yi feel very guilty and sorry for his wife.

One day, when he noticed that his wife got grey hair, he blamed himself even more. When he thought of the medicine of immortality hidden by the Queen Mother of the West on Mount Kunlun in the west, he went through forty-nine hurdles and nine deaths to get the medicine from the Queen Mother. She told him that the medicine would ensure that he and his wife would live forever, and that if a man took it, he could ascend to heaven and become immortal. He thanked the Queen Mother and gave the medicine to his wife for safekeeping, agreeing to eat the medicine together the next day after paying respect to his ancestors on the 15th day of the 8th month. But little did he know that his conversation with the wife would be overheard by Feng Meng, a villain with evil intentions.

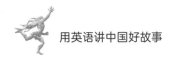

The next day, when Yi wanted to take his disciples out to practice archery, Feng Meng stayed behind on the pretext that he was sick and forced Chang'e to hand over the medicine. She pretended not to know, but he told her about his **eavesdropping** and wanted to search her body forcibly. Seeing that the medicine was about to be **snatched away** by him, she was forced to swallow it and felt like she was flying. She couldn't bear to leave Yi and flew towards the moon, living alone in the lunar palace, longing to be reunited with her husband one day.

eavesdropping
n. 偷听

snatch away
抢走

TIPS: The story of "Chang'e Flying to the Moon" is originated from the worship of the stars by the ancients, and was first recorded in the *Huainanzi* and other ancient books. In 2004, China officially launched a lunar exploration project and named it Chang'e Project, and the artificial satellites orbiting the moon were also named after Chang'e, such as Chang'e-1 and Chang'e-2, etc.

逢蒙杀羿

嫦娥奔月后，羿把更多精力用在收徒和传授箭术上，希望后继有人。

逢蒙是箭术最好、最受羿喜欢的弟子。他在威逼师母嫦娥奔月之后，把自己完美地伪装起来，更加用心地侍候师傅，骗得羿对他的信任。羿把自己的本领毫无保留地都传授给了这位徒弟，希望他将来把箭术发扬光大。

转眼两年过去了，逢蒙在师傅羿的精心教导下，箭术已经可以和师傅相提并论。羿为徒弟感到自豪，逢蒙内心却生出虚荣和妒忌。这天，羿带领众徒弟外出练箭，恰好天上有雁群飞过。逢蒙心想挑战师傅的机会来了，便对着雁群连发三箭，只见三只头部中箭的大雁先后坠地。羿见了很开心，便也射出三支箭，他射中的三只大雁，每一支箭都从大雁两只眼穿过。逢蒙见了才知与羿的差距，想要超过师傅，不知还需要再练多少年。顿时，恶向胆边生，想杀师傅取而代之。

一天，羿外出办事归来，途中忽见树林中"嗖嗖"地飞出一支支冷箭。羿手疾眼快，也射出一支支箭，与那冷箭相撞。当十支冷箭都被羿挡下后，羿才看清杀他的竟然是他最爱的徒弟逢蒙。这时逢蒙又搭上一支箭，要置师傅于死地，而羿手中的箭已经用完了！当箭射过来时，羿来不及躲闪，从马上滚落下来。

逢蒙得意大笑，直奔过来想看看师傅死去的模样，只见羿突然翻身坐起，把逢蒙吓得半死。羿吐出口中的箭镞，苦笑道："难道'啮镞法'（用牙齿把箭头叼住的方法）都忘了吗？"逢蒙吓得立马跪在师傅面前苦苦求饶，声称只是开个玩笑，想偷偷测试一下师傅的反应力和箭术。羿善良宽厚，觉得逢蒙是个人才，应给他改过自新的机会，便原谅了他。

此后，逢蒙伪装悔过自新，无时无刻不在寻找机会；而羿对爱徒却深信不疑，一点提防也没有。这天，羿正在瞄准猎物时，逢蒙操起预先准备好的

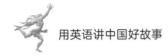

木棍,突然朝他脑后砸去……

为民造福的英雄,就这样死在了徒弟的手下。

【阅读小贴士】英雄羿的悲剧是他没有看清他最喜爱的徒弟逢蒙的真面目,这也启示人们:为人师者,不仅要教技术,同时更要教德行,也就是今天说的教书育人。

Yi Murdered by Feng Meng

After Chang'e flew to the moon, the hero Yi devoted more of his energy to accept apprentices and teach them the archery, hoping for a successor.

Feng Meng was the best archer and the most loved apprentice by Yi. After he had forced his master's wife Chang'e to fly to the moon, he **disguised** perfectly and served his master more attentively to deceive Yi into trusting him. Yi taught his disciple all his skills, hoping that he would be able to develop the archery skills in the future.

disguise
v. 伪装

Two years had passed and Feng Meng, under the careful instruction of his master Yi, could now match his master in archery skills, while Yi was proud of his disciple, Feng Meng grew vain and jealous in his heart. On that day, Yi led his disciples out to practice archery, it happened that a flock of geese flew overhead. Thinking that he had a chance to challenge his master, Feng Meng shot three arrows at the flock of geese, only to see three geese with arrows in their heads falling to the ground one after another. Yi was so happy to see this situation that he also took out three arrows and each of the three arrows he shot passed through both eyes of the geese. When Feng Meng saw his master's archery, he realized the difference

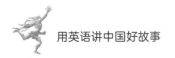

between him and his master, and that he would need many years of practice to surpass his master. Suddenly, he had an evil thought that he wanted to kill his master and replace him.

One day, when Yi was returning from an errand, he suddenly saw cold arrows one by one flying out of the woods. Quick as a flash, he also shot arrows one by one and collided with it. Only when all ten arrows were deflected did he see that his favourite disciple, Feng Meng, was the one who wanted to kill him. At that moment, Feng Meng was ready to kill his master with another arrow, but the arrows in Yi's hand had already been used up! When the arrow came, he was too late to dodge and rolled off his horse.

Feng Meng laughed in triumph and ran straight over to see how dead his master looked, only to see his master suddenly roll over and sit up, scaring him half to death. His master spat out the arrowhead in his mouth and said with a bitter smile, "Have you forgotten the arrowhead-engaging method (hold the arrows in one's teeth)?" Feng Meng was so frightened that he immediately knelt down in front of his master and begged for forgiveness, saying that he was just joking and wanted to test his master's reflection and archery skills secretly. Yi was kind and generous and felt that his disciple was a talented man and should be given a chance to reform, so he forgave him.

Thereafter, Feng Meng disguised his repentance and looked for opportunities all the time; while Yi trusted his

beloved disciple and took no precautions. One day, when the master was aiming at the prey, his disciple picked up a pre-prepared wooden stick and suddenly smashed it at the back of his head...

A hero who had brought benefits to the people died at the hands of his apprentice.

TIPS: The tragedy of the hero Yi was that he did not see the true nature of his favorite disciple Feng Meng, which also inspired people: a teacher should not only teach skills but also teach moral conduct, which is today called imparting knowledge and educating people.

河伯与宓妃

传说宓妃是东方木德之帝伏羲的女儿，溺亡于洛水，成了洛神。她"翩若惊鸿，婉若游龙，荣耀秋菊，华茂春松"，美得无与伦比。

洛河两岸景色迷人，那里居住着一个勤劳勇敢的民族，叫做有洛氏部落。宓妃慕名来到这里，教有洛氏百姓结网捕鱼，传授他们狩猎、养畜、放牧的好方法。

居住在黄河里的河神河伯，听说洛河两岸景色迷人，也来到洛河看看，见到宓妃正在河边教人们结网捕鱼。河伯一下子就被她的美貌迷住了。于是，河伯化在洛河里掀起轩然大波，吞没了水边的宓妃。

河伯把宓妃带入水府深宫，威逼与他结婚成家。婚后不久，宓妃忍受不了河伯的虚伪和残忍——每年都要从人间挑选美女做他新娘，不答应他的要求，就要兴风作浪，发洪水淹没村庄，害人性命。宓妃逃离河伯，悄悄回到了洛河。她要保护洛河里不再有无辜少女被淹死，做洛河两岸居民的保护神。

【阅读小贴士】宓妃被誉为洛水女神，有一颗善良而勇敢的心。

Hebo and Fufei

Legend has it that Fufei was the daughter of Fuxi, the Emperor of Wood in the east, who drowned in the Luo River and became the goddess of that river. She was unparalleled in beauty: "Fluttering like a stunning diva, graceful as a wandering dragon, glorious as an autumn chrysanthemum, luxuriant as a spring pine."

The scenery on both banks of the Luo River was enchanting, and there lived a hard-working and brave people called the You Luo tribe. Fufei came here in admiration and taught the people in the tribe to make nets for fishing, and taught them good methods of hunting, animal breeding and herding.

The river god Hebo, who lived in the Yellow River, heard about the fascinating scenery on the banks of the Luo River and came to see it, where he saw Fufei teaching people how to make nets for fishing. He was instantly enchanted by her beauty. Therefore, the river god made a huge storm in the Luo River and **engulfed** Fufei at the water's edge.

engulf

v. 包围；吞没

Hebo took Fufei into the deep water palace and forced her to marry him and start a family. Soon after the marriage, she could not stand the **hypocrisy** and cruelty of her husband—every year he would choose a beautiful

hypocrisy

n. 虚伪

woman from the earth to be his bride, and if she did not agree to his demands, he would make a storm and flood the village, killing people. She escaped from her husband and quietly returned to the Luo River. She wanted to protect the Luo River from the drowning of innocent girls and to be the protector of the inhabitants on both sides of the river.

TIPS: Fufei is known as the goddess of the Luo River and has a kind and brave heart.

洛水女神

离开河伯的宓妃,独自在洛水过着清贫的生活,两岸勤劳的百姓成了她永远也看不够的风景。夜晚寂寞的时候,她便一个人静静坐在岸边为善良的人们祈福。

一天,射日英雄羿追逐一只羚羊,来到洛滨。这是一只受伤的小羚羊,羿没有射杀它的意思,而是替它拔掉身上的箭,爱抚着它,安慰着它,替它疗伤。原来它身上的箭并不是羿留下的,他是在救助那只可怜的小羚羊。最后,他放走了小羚羊,自己却疲惫不堪地靠在一棵树下睡着了。

羿对小羚羊所做的一切,宓妃看得清楚明白。她认出他就是自己一直崇拜的那个侠骨热血的射日英雄。

宓妃情不自禁地现身走近羿,而睡梦中的羿,仍能耳听八方,当四目相对时,双方一见钟情。

羿与宓妃相爱的消息很快传到了河伯耳里,他恼羞成怒,化作一条白龙潜入洛河,掀起风雨,要吞噬洛水两岸的一切。羿搭箭怒射,射中了河伯的左眼,河伯仓皇而逃。

河伯自知不是羿的对手,就跑到天帝那儿告状,天帝早已洞察一切,哈哈大笑,劝告河伯:你无端生害,反而深受其害,得反思自己的行为。河伯自知理亏,回来后再也不敢找羿与宓妃的麻烦了。

从此,羿与宓妃在洛水边居住下来,过上了美满幸福的生活。人们尊羿为宗布神,尊宓妃为洛神。

【阅读小贴士】神仙的生活其实是世俗百姓生活的写照。神话中塑造的洛神形象,给今人启示,女性解放当自强,敢恨敢爱,勇敢追求自己的美好生活。

Goddess of Luo River

After leaving Hebo, Fufei lived a life of poverty alone in the Luo River, where the hard-working people on both banks became a sight she could never get enough of. At night, when she was lonely, she would sit alone on the shore and pray for the kind people.

One day, Yi, the hero who shot down the nine surplus suns, chased an antelope and came near the Luo River. It was a wounded young antelope. Instead of shooting it, he **plucked** the arrows from its body, caressed it, comforted it and healed its wounds. It turned out that the arrow was not left by him, and he was rescuing the poor little antelope. Finally, he let the little antelope go, but he was exhausted and fell asleep under a tree.

What he had done to the little antelope was seen clearly by Fufei. She recognized him as the **chivalrous**, bloodthirsty sun-shooting hero she had always admired.

She couldn't help but appear to approach him, who still kept his ears to the ground in his sleep, and when their eyes met, both of them fall in love at first sight.

The news of Yi and Fufei's love soon reached the ears of Hebo, who became enraged and dived into the Luo River as a white dragon, raising a storm that would swallow up everything on both sides of the river. Yi shot

pluck
v. 拔掉

chivalrous
adj. 彬彬有礼的

an arrow with anger and hit him in the left eye, and he fled in haste.

He knew that he couldn't defeat Yi, so he ran to the Emperor of Heaven to complain. The emperor had already seen everything and laughed loudly, advising him that he should reflect on his actions, as he caused harm for no reason but was harmed by it. Knowing that he was in the wrong, Hebo came back and dared not trouble Hou Yi and Fufei again.

From then on, Yi and Fufei lived down by the water of Luo River and lived a nice and happy life. Yi was worshipped as the God of Zongbu and Fufei as the Goddess of Luo River.

TIPS: The life of the immortals is in fact a reflection of the life of the common people. The mythological image of the Goddess of Luo River has inspired today's people that women should be **emancipated** to be self-empowered, dare to hate and love, and bravely pursue their own good lives.

emancipate

v. 解放

吴刚伐树

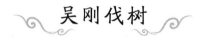

相传月宫中长着一棵桂树,高达五百多丈,枝繁叶茂,非常粗壮。树下有个叫吴刚的人,长年累月在挥动斧头砍伐它。每当他累了,稍作停顿,就会有鸟儿飞过来,朝被砍处啄上一口,然后瞬间愈合。吴刚只好重新去砍,树又接着愈合。这样周而复始,年复一年,这棵桂树仍没有被他砍倒。

明知桂树不可能被砍断,那吴刚为何还要砍下去?

吴刚本是民间樵夫,但他不安心做樵夫,只想着做神仙。想做神仙的吴刚,怎么又跑到月球上伐树去了呢?

原来,吴刚在拜仙学艺中,发现成仙之路更加艰难,他受不了那种苦,三年换了三个师傅,仍一无所获,最后没有人愿意收他为徒,流落街头,晕倒在地,被一位白发老者救了。吴刚再次拜老者学习仙术,总算学到一些皮毛,就得意忘形,偷偷使用仙术隐身,去做偷盗钱财的坏事。老者觉得自己救错了人,决定要惩罚徒弟,不让他留在人间继续危害他人。

老者将吴刚带到月宫,给了他一把斧子,叫他去砍那棵桂树,并嘱咐他:"这是你改过自新的机会,也是你修炼成仙的机会。砍倒桂树,你就能得道成仙。"

吴刚看着面前高达五百丈的桂树,想起愚公移山的故事,相信只要一天天砍下去,总有被砍倒的一天。就这样,吴刚便挥起斧头砍树,没想到被砍的地方总能自动愈合,让他前功尽弃。他由最初的气愤、失望,变得不甘心。一年年下来,他变得平和起来,意外发现自己年轻了,浑身有使不完的劲。每年桂花盛开,随着他的砍伐震动桂树,桂花播散到人间,馨香四溢,人间有了桂花糕和桂花月饼这样的美食。他看着一家家团圆喜乐的幸福场景,觉得自己的劳动有了不同的意义,于是不停地砍下去,直到今天。

【阅读小贴士】吴刚不安分守己,想做神仙,在修仙过程中犯了错,被罚去月宫砍树。在砍树过程中,吴刚的心情也在变化之中,可见心态决定状态,状态决定成败。吴刚能不能成仙,已经不重要了,重要的是吴刚在无休止的砍树过程中,悟到了自己存在的价值和意义。人生也如此。

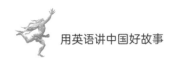

Wu Gang Cutting the Laurel

According to legend, there was a **laurel** growing in the Moon Palace, more than 500 *zhang* high, with luxuriant branches and leaves, very thick. There was a man named Wu Gang under the tree who spent years and years swinging his axe to cut it down. Whenever he got tired and paused, a bird would fly over and peck at the chopped place, which then instantly healed. He had to go back to cut, and the tree then healed. Week after week, year after year, the laurel was still not cut down by him.

Knowing that the tree could not be cut down, why did he keep on cutting it down?

He was originally a folk woodcutter, but he was not satisfied as a woodcutter, only thinking about being an immortal. How did Wu Gang, who wanted to be an immortal, go to the moon to cut the tree?

It turned out that in the process of his worshiping of immortals to learn the skills, he found the road to immortality more difficult and could not stand that kind of suffering. He changed three masters in three years, but still learned nothing. In the end, no one was willing to take him as a disciple, and he fell down on the street and was saved by a white-haired old man. He learned the immortality from the old man again, and when he finally learned a

laurel

n. 月桂

few things, he got carried away and secretly used his immortality to become invisible and went about the bad business of stealing money. Feeling that he had saved the wrong person, the old man decided to punish his disciple and prevent him from staying on the earth to continue to harm others.

The old man took him to the Moon Palace, gave him an axe and told him to chop down the laurel, and instructed him, "This is your chance to reform and to train to become an immortal. Cut down the laurel and you will become immortal."

Looking at the laurel, which was five hundred *zhang* high in front of him, he remembered the story of *Yu Gong Removing Mountains* and believed that if he kept cutting it day by day, it would be chopped down one day. Then he swung his axe and cut the tree, but to his surprise, the area that had been cut would always heal itself, leaving his previous efforts in vain. From his initial anger and disappointment, he became resigned to the situation. As the years went by, he became peaceful again and unexpectedly found himself younger, with an **inexhaustible** energy. Each year the laurel bloomed, and as his cutting shook the trees, the flowers spread to the earth, the fragrance was **diffused** all around, and laurel cake and laurel moon-cakes became delicacies in the world. He also saw the happy scene of a family reunion and joy, and felt that his labour had a different meaning, so he kept on cutting the laurel until today.

inexhaustible
adj. 无穷无尽的

diffuse
v. 扩散；弥散

TIPS: Wu Gang was restless and wanted to be an immortal. He made a mistake during his immortal training and was punished to go to the Moon Palace to cut the laurel. In the process of chopping down the tree, his mood was also in the process of changing, which shows that the state of mind determines the state and the state determines success or failure. It is no longer important whether he can become an immortal or not. What is important is that he realizes the value and meaning of his existence in the endless process of cutting the laurel. So it is with life.

舜离家出走

舜是父系氏族社会后期部落联盟的首领,"三皇五帝"之一,因他每只眼睛里都有两个瞳子,又名重华,号有虞氏,史称虞舜。

舜的父亲瞽(gǔ)叟是个瞎老头,却是帝颛顼的五世孙,那么舜就是帝颛顼的六世孙了。在舜出生前,瞽叟做了个奇怪的梦,梦见一只凤凰衔着米来喂他,说他是来给他做子孙的。不久,她的原配妻子握登就生下儿子,取名叫舜。

舜在很小的时候,母亲就因病去世了。不久舜的父亲再娶,舜的后娘生了个儿子叫象,生了个女儿叫敤(kě)首。

舜的后娘是个极其阴毒的女人,在她刚嫁过来时,只在私下里变着花样偷偷折磨舜,让他干重活,不给饭吃、罚他站着睡觉。等她生下一双儿女后,更是把舜看成眼中钉,明目张胆地虐待舜,想置他于死地。舜的父亲瞽叟年迈眼盲,是个"糊涂虫""妻管严",不但没能保护舜,还跟着一起打骂舜。父母尚且如此,弟妹们更是不给做大哥的一点情面。舜心里明白,这个家已经容不下他了,他只好逃走。

【阅读小贴士】舜被后母虐待的故事在很多后母型童话故事里都可以看到,这里不仅仅有人性自私与恶的问题,还有人与社会的道德问题,而后母虐待非亲生子女的结果,都是坚持了善恶终有报的逻辑,坚信真善美必将战胜假恶丑。

Shun Escaping from Home

Shun was a legendary leader of ancient China in the late patrilineal society, regarded as one of the Three Sovereigns and Five Emperors. He was also known as "Chonghua" because he had two pupils in each eye. He was also known as You Yu or called as Yu Shun in Chinese history.

His father Gusou was a blind old man, but a fifth-generation grandson of Emperor Zhuanxü, so Shun would be a sixth-generation grandson of Zhuanxü. Before he was born, his father had a strange dream that a phoenix came to feed him with rice in its mouth, saying that he came to become his descendant. Soon afterwards, his original wife, Wodeng, gave birth to a son, who was named "Shun".

When he was very young, his mother died of illness. Soon afterwards, his father remarried, and his stepmother then gave birth to Shun's half brother Xiang and half sister Keshou.

His stepmother was an extremely **sinister** woman. While she was first married, she only abused Shun in many ways in private and in secret, making him do heavy work, refusing to give him food and punishing him for sleeping on his feet. When she gave birth to her son and daughter, she saw Shun as a thorn in her side and **blatantly** abused

sinister
adj. 邪恶的

blatantly
adv. 公然地

him, trying to kill him. His father, being blind and eldely, was a "scatterbrain" and a "hen-pecked husband" who not only failed to protect him, but also followed his wife in scolding him. With his parents treating him badly, his siblings did not show any mercy to him as an elder brother. He knew in his heart that there was no more room for him in the family and he had to run away.

TIPS: The story of Shun being abused by his stepmother can be found in many stepmother-type fairy tales. Here there is not only the problem of human selfishness and evil, but also the moral problems of people and society. And the result of the stepmother's abuse of her non-biological children is that it adheres to the logic that what goes around, comes around, believing that the truthfulness, kindness and beauty will defeat the fault, ugliness and evil.

舜德行天下

少年舜逃出了家,无处安身,就在历山脚下搭建了一间毛草房,自己开垦荒地种谷物,饿了就吃树叶、啃树皮。生活虽然非常困苦,却不再挨打、挨骂,日子倒也自由自在,苦中有乐。

历山脚下的农民,经常为争地界吵架。舜就劝说他们:何必为一点点土地伤了和气,你们可以到历山脚下,我们一起开垦土地自己种。舜还拿出自己辛苦开垦的土地,让给没有土地的人。在舜的德行感化下,人们也学会了彼此谦让,大家一起到野外开荒种地。

舜带领人们去捕鱼、打猎,经常有惊人的收获,每次舜都把所得公平地分给大家,自己只取最少的那一份。人们对他既敬佩又爱戴,跟随舜的人也越来越多。后来那些人又跟着舜去黄河之滨烧制陶器,还跟着他在顿丘一带学着经商做生意。舜又将他们组织起来,分工合作,有条不紊,各得其所,各得其乐,仅两三年时间,舜的茅草房周边聚集成了一个村落。

舜在帮助别人的同时,自己的日子也红火起来。他经常把自己的劳动所得,毫无保留地送去孝敬父母,对他们曾经的虐待毫无怨言。遇上荒年,舜还拿出钱粮接济父母。舜到二十岁时,他的德行与孝心已经名扬天下。

后来,帝尧选继承人,舜被四岳推荐给帝尧,帝尧为了考验他,把两个女儿嫁给了他。舜不但把家庭关系处理得好,而且在各方面都表现出卓越的才干和高尚的人格魅力。

舜以他的德行与孝心改变了自己的人生命运。

【阅读小贴士】少年舜的故事非常励志,人在逆境中如何生活,这是很好的案例。舜以德行去感化了身边的人,他自己最后是最大的受益者,此所谓善有善报。

Shun's Virtue to the World

When the young Shun escaped from home and had nowhere to stay, he built a straw hut at the foot of Mount Li and cleared the land to grow the grain, eating leaves and chewing on tree bark when he was hungry. Although his life was very difficult, he was no longer beaten or scolded, and his life was free and happy in spite of his suffering.

The farmers at the foot of Mount Li often quarreled over the boundaries of their land. He persuaded them that there was no need to break the peace over a little land. He advised that they could go to the bottom of the mountain and clear the land to grow the grain together. He also gave out the land he had worked hard to cultivate and gave it to those who had no land. Under the influence of his virtue, the people learned to be humble to each other and went out into the wilderness to cultivate the land and grow the grain together.

He led the people on fishing and hunting, and often had amazing harvests. Each time he shared the proceeds fairly with everyone, taking only the smallest share himself. The people both admired and loved him, and more and more people followed him. Later, those people followed Shun to the shores of the Yellow River to fire pottery, and also followed him around Dunqiu to learn how

to do business. Shun organized them all again, dividing the work into an orderly manner, and each was in his proper place. In only two or three years, a village gathered around his straw hut.

While helping others, Shun's own life was also prosperous. He often gave the proceeds of his labour to his parents without reservation, and had no complaints about the abuse they had once inflicted on him. When there was a bad year, he even gave money and food to help his parents. By the time he reached the age of twenty, his virtue and **filial piety** had become famous throughout the world.

Later, when Emperor Yao chose his successor, he was recommended to him by Si Yue, and the emperor married his two daughters to him at the same time in order to test him. He not only managed his family relations well, but also showed outstanding talent and noble character in all aspects.

With his virtue and filial piety, he changed his destiny in life.

filial piety
孝道

TIPS: The story of the young Shun is a very inspiring example of how people live in adversity. Shun used his virtue to influence those people around him, and he became the greatest beneficiary in the end. This was called: Doing good will cause good to return.

舜孝行天下

尧帝选择舜作为接班人人选后，把自己的两个女儿嫁给他为妻，还赐给舜财富。舜没有因为做了尧的女婿、变富贵了，就骄傲起来，相反，他比过去更加谦卑。

成家后，舜准备了礼物，带着妻子回去看望父母和弟弟妹妹，好像他们根本没有虐待过他。他的两个妻子也平易近人，孝顺公婆，和睦邻里。舜的弟弟象嫉妒舜拥有的一切，和舜的后母密谋要杀死舜，挑唆舜的父亲也一起参与。一个杀害舜的毒计，就这样由舜"最亲的家人"设计出来了。

这一天，弟弟象过来传话：父亲让舜去帮忙修谷仓。舜把这件事告诉了两个妻子。两妻子怀疑他的父母及弟弟是想借修谷仓把舜活活烧死！于是妻子女英提醒他一定要小心，妻子娥皇拿出一件鸟纹衣服说："赶紧脱掉你的旧衣服，穿这件鸟纹衣服去……"

舜便穿了新衣服去修谷仓。当时他并没有把妻子的话听进去，因为他认为童年的遭遇都已成为过去了，这些年自己一直孝顺父母，也没有冲突，他们不至于要置他于死地。可他想错了，他刚爬上谷仓顶，下面的梯子就被搬走了。不一会儿四周燃起熊熊大火。舜惊呆了，滚滚浓烟向他扑来，他以为自己要被烧死了。最后，他张开双臂向着苍天大喊："怎么办啊，我还有好多要做的事情没有做啊！"说也奇怪，就在他张开双臂的一刹那间，舜在冲天火光中，变成一只五彩大鸟，腾空飞走了，让要害舜性命的人目瞪口呆。

【阅读小贴士】这些也算是对舜孝心和他们夫妻情感的考验吧。妒忌会让人心变得险恶，亲情变得无情。

Shun's Filial Piety to the World

After Emperor Yao chose Shun as his successor, he married his two daughters to him and gave him wealth. Shun did not become **arrogant** although he was Yao's son-in-law and had become rich, rather he was more humble than ever.

When he became a family man, he prepared gifts and took his wives back to visit his parents and younger siblings, as if they had not mistreated him at all. His two wives were also easy-going, dutiful to their in-laws and harmonious with their neighbours. Shun's half brother and stepmother became extremely jealous of everything he had and **conspired** to kill him, instigating his father to join in. A poisonous plan to kill Shun was devised by Shun's "closest family members".

One day, Xiang came over with a message that his father had asked Shun to help repair the barn. He told his two wives about the message. The two wives suspected that his parents and half brother wanted to use the excuse of repairing the barn to burn him alive! So his wife, Nüying, reminded him that he must be careful, and his wife, Ehuang, took out a bird-print **garment** and said, "Hurry up. Take off your old clothes and put on this bird-print garment and go…"

arrogant
adj. 傲慢的；自大的

conspire
v. 图谋；密谋

garment
n. 衣服

神话故事

Then he put on his new clothes and went to repair the barn. He did not take his wife's words to heart at the time, for he thought that all his childhood encounters were in the past, that he had been dutiful to his parents all these years, and that there had been no conflict, and that they were not so intent on causing him death. But he was wrong. He had just climbed to the top of the barn when the ladder below was removed. Within moments a roaring fire was burning all around. He was stunned as the smoke rolled towards him and he thought he was going to be burnt to death. At last he opened his arms to the sky and cried out, "What shall I do? I have so much to do that I have not yet done!" Strangely enough, the very moment he opened his arms, he turned into a big colourful bird in the rushing fire and flew away in the air, leaving the people who wanted to kill his life stunned.

TIPS: These were sort of tests of Shun's filial piety and their emotions as a couple. Jealousy has a way of poisoning the heart. It would make your heart sinister and the kinship unfeeling.

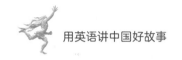

舜变金龙

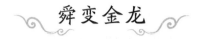

一计不成,又生一计。

几天后,舜的父亲来求舜,说家中院子里的那口井水浑浊了,让舜第二天上午帮他淘一下;并声称之前那场火灾是个意外,让舜不要记恨他们。

舜送走父亲,两位妻子觉得不妥,就连夜赶回娘家,向父亲帝尧求救,然后借回来一件龙纹衣服。

第二天,舜把那件龙纹衣服贴身穿在里面,外面罩上平时穿的衣服,就赶回父亲家里。家里人看见舜没有穿上次那种奇装异服,便暗暗高兴。弟弟象用一根事先准备好的粗绳系在舜的腰上,然后把舜从井口放下去,还没下到井底,绳子便被割断了。舜"砰"地一声掉进井里。

这时,舜想起妻子的嘱咐,迅速脱下外衣,口中默念妻子教他的咒语,顿时自己变成了一条金龙,从井旁边潜遁出去了。舜看见自己的继母和弟弟象正忙着用石头及泥块把井口封起来呢。

所有人都认为舜这次必死无疑。继母和弟弟以送信为名赶到舜家里,其实是要瓜分他家的财产。象的妹妹实在看不下去了,质问、谴责他们:"你们这样做就不怕遭报应吗?"

"什么报应啊?"这时,只见舜从外面从容不迫地走了进来。舜的继母及弟弟象以为"活见鬼"了,吓得直接跪地求饶,善良的舜再一次原谅了他们。

【阅读小贴士】舜以德报怨,与继母及弟弟的恶毒行为形成鲜明对比,善恶分明。舜每一次都能脱离危险,都与妻子的提醒和切实帮助分不开。平凡的人借用宝物——龙纹衣保护自己脱离危险,表明舜的故事已经开始了从历史神话向传说童话转型,神与人的形象更生活化。

Shun Turning into Golden Dragon

When one plan failed, another plan was born.

A few days later, Shun's father came to beg him, saying that the well in the family yard was muddy and that he should help him pluck it next day; he also claimed that the previous fire had been an accident and asked Shun not to hold a **grudge** against them.

grudge

n. 积怨；怨恨

When Shun sent his father away, his two wives were not calm. Sensing that his father came with viciousness, they rushed back to their mother's home overnight and asked their father Emperor Yao for help, borrowing back a dragon print garment.

The next day, Shun wore the dragon garment close to his body, with his usual clothes over it, and rushed back to his father's home. The family was secretly happy to see that he was not wearing the same strange costume as last time. Shun's half brother Xiang tied a pre-prepared thick rope to his waist and lowered him down the well, but the rope was cut before he reached the bottom. He fell into the well with a **thud**.

thud

n. 砰的一声

Remembering his wives' instructions at this time, he quickly took off his coat and mouthed the incantation they had taught him, turning himself into a golden dragon and diving out of the well. He saw his stepmother and half

brother Xiang busy sealing the mouth of the well with rocks and mud blocks.

Everyone thought that he would surely die this time. His stepmother and half brother rushed to his house under the pretext of delivering a letter, but in fact they wanted to divide up his family's property. Xiang's younger sister couldn't stand it anymore and condemned them, "Aren't you afraid of **retribution** for making this behavior?"

"What retribution?" At that moment, Shun was seen coming in from outside in a calm and unhurried manner. His stepmother and half brother Xiang thought they had seen a ghost and were so frightened that they knelt down and begged for forgiveness. Once again, the kind Shun forgave them.

retribution

n. 严惩；报应

TIPS: Shun returned good for evil, in contrast to the vicious behavior of his stepmother and half brother, where good and evil are clearly distinguished. At every turn, his ability to get out of danger was inseparable from his wives' warnings and practical help. The fact that the common people borrowed the treasure—the dragon print garment, to protect themselves from danger suggests that the story of Shun has begun its transition from historical myth to legendary fairy tale, with a more lifelike portrayal of god and human.

舜传位给禹

　　帝舜接替帝尧的王位后，让四岳推荐贤才来一起参与治理国家。被推荐的人都经过舜的考核，彼此能互相谦让。帝舜整顿礼制，在民间进行教化推动，要求人民"行厚德，远佞人"，树立礼仪规范。舜任命典乐官员，要求做到教育贵族弟子正直温和，宽厚严厉，刚正不暴虐，简捷不傲慢，达到八音协调一致，不互相错乱侵扰，神人相和的境界。舜重视民间疾苦灾难，任命禹治水，完成了尧未完成的盛业。后又减轻刑罚，统一度量衡。

　　在舜执政的第二十八年，帝尧去世。舜守孝三年之后，便将王位主动让给尧的儿子丹朱。舜越是这样恭敬谦让，天下诸侯越是敬仰他、维护他。在各诸侯国的一再恳请下，舜又重回帝位，把国家治理得井井有条、繁荣昌盛。

　　舜还是五弦琴的创制者，他还谱写了一首叫《南风》的曲子，闲时会边弹边唱，表达他对人民的热爱："南方吹来温暖的风啊，可以消除我的人民的愁怨啊！南方吹来的应时的风啊，可以增加我的人民的财富啊！"

　　舜在位三十九年，虽有九个儿子，但他仍然把王位留给了治水有功的禹。舜晚年出巡，死在苍梧（今湖南宁远县），葬于九嶷山下。噩耗传来，人民无不痛哭流泪，他的两位爱妻深爱丈夫，双双投湘水自尽，成了传说中的"湘水之神"，称"湘夫人"或"湘妃"。

【阅读小贴士】舜用自己的一生践行了人应有的德行，为万世师表。妻子追随他而去，既有夫妻间感天动地的爱情，为爱殉情；也可能为后世封建社会夫权制度的形成开了不好的头。

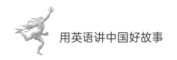

Shun Abdicating the Throne to Yu

After Emperor Shun's reign, he asked four Mount Gods to recommend wise men to join him in governing the country. All those recommended were tested by him and were able to be humble to each other. Emperor Shun reorganized the ritual system, promoted education among the people, asking them to "practice virtue and distance themselves from sycophants" and established a code of **etiquette**. He appointed music officials to teach the nobles to be righteous and gentle, generous and stern, upright and not tyrannical, simple and not arrogant, and to achieve harmony between the eight tones, not to disturb each other, and to reach the realm of harmony between the god and man. He valued the hardships and disasters the people had encountered and appointed Yu to control floods, completing the work that Emperor Yao had not yet finished. Later, he reduced penalties and standardized weights and measures.

In the 28th year of his reign, Emperor Yao died. After waiting for Yao's three years of mourning to be completed, he voluntarily ceded the crown to Yao's son Danzhu. The more respectful and humbler he was, the more the lords of the world looked up to him and stuck up for him. After repeated pleas from the lords, he returned to the throne and

etiquette

n. 礼节；规矩

神话故事

ruled the country in good order and prosperity.

He was also the creator of the **five-stringed zither**. He also composed a tune called "The South Wind", which he would play and sing in his spare time, expressing his love for his people: "O warm wind from the south, which can dispel the sorrows of my people! O wind that blows in time from the south to increase the wealth of my people!"

He reigned for thirty-nine years, and although he had nine sons, he still abdicated the throne to Yu, who made contributions when controlling floods. In his later years, Shun went on a tour and died in Cangwu (now Ningyuan County, Hunan Province). He was buried at the bottom of Jiuyi Mount, and all the people wept when the sad news came. His two beloved wives loved their husbands so much that they both threw themselves into the Xiang River and became the legendary "Goddesses of Xiang River", known as "Lady Xiang" or "Concubine Xiang".

TIPS: Shun spent his life practising the virtues expected of a man and was a teacher for all ages. His wife followed him, both in the form of a touching love between husband and wife, **martyred** for love, and possibly in the form of a bad start for the formation of the marital power system in later feudal society.

five-stringed zither
五弦琴

martyr
v. 使殉难

湘妃竹的传说

岳阳的君山岛被誉为爱情岛,只因岛上长有一种湘妃竹。在湘妃竹的背后有一段凄美的故事。

相传在帝舜执政晚年,湖南九嶷山一带因小部落之间战乱,引发九条恶龙作怪,导致洪水冲毁百姓庄稼和房屋。帝舜得知后,决定亲自到南方督战,平服战乱,惩治恶龙。

帝舜的两位夫人娥皇和女英不放心他独自远行,请求陪同前往。帝舜深知此行险恶,不想让她们涉险,便偷偷启程了。

帝舜走后,娥皇和女英只有祈祷帝舜早日凯旋。可左等右等,没有消息,她们决定去寻找帝舜,途经洞庭湖时,恰遇大风,便在洞庭岛上停歇。不久,她们收到帝舜已驾崩于九嶷山的噩耗。她们顿觉天旋地转,悲痛欲绝,抱着路边翠竹痛哭。泪水打落在竹竿上,顿时形成擦不掉也抹不去的黑色泪斑。一夜之间,那满山的翠竹,仿佛也在陪着她们哭泣,染上了斑斑泪痕。

第三天,两位夫人强忍悲伤,启程前往九嶷山。她们见到了环绕在翠竹间的帝舜墓。听乡亲们说,帝舜平了战乱、斩了恶龙后,自己却累病了,再也没能起来。娥皇和女英抱着坟前翠竹再次痛哭,眼泪洒在了九嶷山的竹竿上,同样呈现出点点泪斑,有紫色的,有雪白的,还有血红色的。九天九夜后,哭干了眼泪的两位夫人双双投入湘水,化作湘水之神,称"湘夫人"或"湘妃"。

为了纪念她们,人们把洞庭山改为君山,把染上泪斑的竹子称为"湘妃竹"。

【阅读小贴士】"湘妃竹"借物抒情,赞美忠贞不渝的美好爱情。舜帝的故事到这里也就告一段落了。

神话故事

Legend of Mottled Bamboo

Junshan Island in Yueyang is also known as Love Island, simply because of the mottled bamboo that grows on the island. There is a **poignant** story behind the Mottled Bamboo.

According to legend, in the late years of Emperor Shun's reign, a war between small tribes around Mount Jiuyi in Hunan caused nine evil dragons to come out and cause floods that destroyed the people's crops and houses. When Emperor Shun learned of this, he decided to go to the south and supervise the war in person to **quell** the war and punish the dragons.

Emperor Shun's two wives, Ehuang and Nüying, were worried about him travelling alone and asked to accompany him. Knowing the dangers of such a trip, Shun did not want to put them at risk, so he set off in secret.

After his departure, Ehuang and Nüying could only pray for his early triumph. They waited for a long time, but there was no news. They decided to look for their husband, but when they passed by Dongting Lake, they encountered a strong wind and stopped at Dongting Island for a rest. Soon after, they received the sad news that their husband had died on Mount Jiuyi. They were so **distraught** that they hugged the bamboos on the roadside and cried. The

poignant
adj. 令人沉痛的；悲惨的

quell
v. 平息；制止

distraught
adj. 心烦意乱的

167

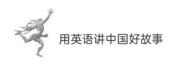

tears fell on the bamboo stalks, forming the black tear mottles that could not be wiped away or erased. Overnight, the mountain of bamboos seemed to be crying with them, stained with tear mottles.

On the third day, the two ladies held back their grief and set off on their journey to Mount Jiuyi. At last they saw the tomb of Emperor Shun surrounded by green bamboos. They were told by the villagers that the emperor had pacified the war and killed the dragon, but that he had fallen ill and never got up again. His two wives hugged the bamboos in front of the tomb and cried again. The tears spilled onto the bamboo stalks of Mount Jiuyi, also showing spots of tears, some purple, some snowy white and some blood red. After nine days and nine nights, the two ladies, who had dried their tears, both plunged into the Xiang River and became the goddesses of it, known as "Lady Xiang" or "Concubine Xiang".

To commemorate them, people changed the name of Mount Dongting to Mount Jun, and the bamboo stained with tear mottles was renamed "Mottled Bamboo".

TIPS: The story of Emperor Shun comes to an end with the Mottled Bamboo, a beautiful tribute to loyalty and love.

鲧偷土治水

尧在位时期，经常发生大洪水，泛滥成灾，百姓无处安生。帝尧寝食难安，招来四岳等人商讨对策，在派谁去治水上，出乎尧所料，大家一致推荐鲧。

鲧，帝颛顼之子，禹的父亲，崇部落的首领。据传他原本是个天神，是黄帝的后代，黄帝生了骆明，骆明生了白马，这匹白马神就是鲧。在尧帝印象中，鲧是个刚愎自用之人，难以担当治水这件大事。但是，大家一致推荐，尧勉强同意了，决定给鲧一次机会。

鲧接受任务后，非常同情洪水中无家可归的人们，心急如焚，却不知从何下手，整日闷闷不乐。他收为心腹的一只猫头鹰和乌龟看到主人这个样子，都抢着为主人排忧解难，说："这有什么难的，水来土掩，只要在河上筑起大堤，拦住洪水，水就不会泛滥了。"鲧一想，是这个道理，可到哪里取这些土石来筑大堤呢？猫头鹰献计说："你祖父黄帝那儿有一种'息壤'，那可是宝物，一点点土就可以长成大堤和万丈高山。用这种宝土来治水，还怕阻挡不住洪水？"

鲧听了，觉得这办法好。可他深知祖父天帝的严厉，不会把天庭之宝给他用于治水。迫不得已，鲧决定先偷走祖父的宝贝，等治好了水患，再向天帝负荆请罪。

【阅读小贴士】鲧是中国汉族上古时代神话传说人物，被举荐治水，一定有他过人之处。为救民于洪水中，他不惜冒着触犯"天条"去偷盗圣土，精神可嘉。

Gun Controlling Floods by Stealing Xirang

During the reign of Emperor Yao, there were frequent worldwide floods which caused disasters and the people had no place to live. The emperor had a hard time sleeping and eating, so he summoned four Mountain Gods and others to discuss **countermeasures**, and when it came to who to send to control floods, to Yao's surprise, they all recommended Gun.

Gun, son of Emperor Zhuanxü, father of Yu and head of the Chong tribe. According to legend, he was originally a celestial god, a descendant of Yellow Emperor. The emperor gave birth to Luo Ming, who gave birth to a white horse, and this white horse god was Gun. Emperor Yao was under the impression that Gun was a headstrong and self-willed man who would not be able to take on the important task of controlling floods. However, everyone unanimously recommended and Yao reluctantly agreed and decided to give Gun a chance.

After accepting the task, Gun was very sympathetic to the people who were homeless in the floods, and was so anxious that he didn't know where to start and spent his days moping. When an owl and a **tortoise**, whom he had taken under his wing, saw their master in such a state,

countermeasure

n. 对策

tortoise

n. 龟

they both rushed to solve their master's problems, saying, "What's so difficult about it? When the flood approaches bank up to keep it out? If you build a big embankment on the river to stop the flood, the water will not overflow." He thought about it, this was true, but where could he get soil and stones to build the embankment? The owl said, "Your grandfather, Yellow Emperor, have a magic soil called Xirang (self-growing soil), which is a treasure. Only a little bit of soil can grow into a big embankment and ten-thousand-*zhang*-high mountain. If you use this precious soil to control floods, you won't be afraid of not being able to stop the flood?"

When he heard this method, he thought it was a good idea. But he knew that his grandfather, the Emperor of Heaven, was very strict and would not give him the treasure of heaven to be used for floods control. As a last resort, he decided to steal his grandfather's treasure at first, and then to apologize to him when he had controlled floods.

TIPS: Gun, a mythical and legendary figure from the ancient Chinese Ethic Han, must have had his merits when he was recommended to control floods. In order to save the people from flooding, he risked breaking the Heavenly Rule by stealing the magic soil. The spirit was commendable.

鲧治水失败

息壤是天帝镇守天庭的宝物之一。鲧利用祖父天帝对他的疼爱，几次三番接近息壤，采用偷梁换柱的办法，成功偷拿到息壤。

拿到息壤后，鲧马上来到洪水最严重的吕梁山一带。息壤治水的办法太灵了，只要到洪水泛滥的河边撒下一点息壤，立即就会长出一道高大的堤坝，挡住汹涌的洪水；有积水的地方撒一点点息壤，积水也很快就干了。鲧用息壤治水，又快又好，百姓们欢天喜地返回原地，重建家园。于是，鲧又奔赴其他洪水严重的地方，如法炮制，立竿见影。帝尧庆幸自己听了大臣们的推荐，才没有埋没鲧这样的治水人才。

九年间，鲧奔波在各地洪水频发的地方，一次次利用息壤堵住了洪水，使人民不受洪水困扰。然而，纸包不住火，鲧偷息壤的事情暴露了。黄帝震怒，立即命火神祝融到人间去惩治鲧，杀了鲧，收走了息壤。息壤被收走，这下鲧的治水彻底失败了。被鲧筑起的拦洪大堤，一个个崩塌，洪水如猛兽般呼啸而来，下游老百姓好不容易重建起来的家园和安稳日子，瞬间被洪水吞没了。

因为鲧偷盗圣土的行为，给人间带来了更大的水患和灾难，鲧死不瞑目。传说鲧死后，他的身体化作一条黄龙，跃入羽山近旁的羽渊之中，不见了；他的精魂化作一条虬龙，头上长角，金鳞闪闪，腾空而起，升上了天空，这就是后来的禹。

【阅读小贴士】鲧为治水最终献出了自己的生命，这种牺牲精神是值得肯定的。对于鲧治水失败，科学的解释是方法不当，一味地采取筑坝挡水的简单办法，堵的结果是河床越抬越高，最终造成堤毁人亡的严重后果。

Gun Failing to Control Floods

Xirang was one of the treasures of the Emperor of Heaven to guard the heavenly palace. Gun took advantage of his grandfather's(the Emperor of Heaven) affection for him and approached the magic substance several times. He adopted the method of perpetrating a fraud and got the soil successfully. He never dreamed that his grandson would steal it from under his nose.

After getting the self-expanding soil, Gun immediately went to the area around Lüliang Mountains where the flooding was most severe. The method of using the resting soil to control floods was helpful, just by sprinkling a little bit of it on a flooding river, a tall embankment would immediately grow up to stop the flooding. Where there was standing water, a little bit of resting soil was spread and the water dried up quickly. He used the resting soil to control floods, quickly and well, and the people returned to their homes with great joy and then rebuilt their homes. Then he went on to other places where the flooding was severe and did the same thing with immediate effect. Emperor Yao was glad that he had listened to his ministers' recommendations so that he had not buried such a talented man as Gun.

For nine years, he travelled around the different

flood-prone areas, using the magic soil to stop the floods and keep the people safe from them. However, the paper couldn't cover the fire, and his theft of the magic soil was revealed. Yellow Emperor became quite angry and immediately ordered Zhu Rong, the God of Fire, to punish Gun by killing him and taking away the self-expanding soil. Now, his action of controlling floods was a complete failure. As the resting soil was taken away, the embankments built by Gun to stop floods collapsed one by one, the floods came roaring in like fierce beasts and the homes and peace rebuilt by the people downstream were instantly swallowed up by floods.

Because of Gun's theft of the sacred soil, he brought even greater floods and disasters to the earth. He turned over in his grave. Legend has it that after his death, his body turned into a yellow dragon and leapt into the Abyss Yu near Mount Yu and disappeared; his spirit turned into a **gnarled** dragon with horns on its head and shining golden scales, and leapt up into the sky, which later became Yu.

TIPS: Gun sacrificed his life for the sake of controlling floods, a spirit of self-sacrifice worthy of recognition. The scientific explanation for his failure to control floods is that his methods were inappropriate, and he took the simple approach of building embankments to hold back the water, which resulted in the riverbed getting higher and higher, eventually leading to the serious consequences of the destruction of the embankments and the death of people.

---

flood-prone area
易发洪水的地区

gnarled
adj. 多节的；弯曲的

禹子承父业

相传禹是其父鲧的精魂所化的一条虬龙,他请求天帝黄帝让他继承父亲的遗志,到人间去为百姓治水。天帝对孙子鲧的死一直心存愧疚,对禹的要求既吃惊又感到安慰,不仅马上答应,还赐给他一些圣土息壤,派将应龙前去帮忙。

禹得到黄帝的支持后,率应龙等大大小小的神龙,浩浩荡荡来到人间治水。禹到了人间,变化成一个身材魁梧的大汉,身长九尺有余,大鼻子、大眼睛,口中长着双层的牙齿,耳朵上有三个孔。

传说人间那场大洪水,是水神共工怒撞不周山导致的,共工听说禹要来治水,再次兴风作浪,要给禹一个下马威。禹看到很多人在洪水中葬送了性命,更加坚定了治水的决心。

在开工前,禹在会稽山召开天下群神大会,动员众神支持他的治水行动,一起商讨治水方案。开会时,一个叫防风氏的人,不仅迟到,还对大禹治水持消极态度,散布不利于合作治水的谣言,禹公开处死了防风氏。

处决防风氏,表明了禹治水的决心,严明了纪律,统一思想,为治水扫清了障碍。

【阅读小贴士】鲧禹治水的故事出自《山海经·海内经》等古书记载。禹有为民治水的决心,更有实现决心的坚定行动。禹治水,注意做思想舆论工作,重视发动群众,是治水的成功法宝之一。

Yu Inheriting His Father's Work

According to legend, Yu was a gnarled dragon transformed from the spirit of his father, Gun, who asked the Emperor of Heaven, known as Yellow Emperor, to let him inherit his father's will to continue the difficult task to control floods. The Yellow Emperor, who had always felt guilty about the death of his grandson Gun, was both surprised and comforted by Yu's request. Not only did he immediately agree, but he also gave him some Xirang (magic soil) and sent his general Yinglong (Responding Dragon) to help him.

With the support of Yellow Emperor, the gnarled dragon Yu led Yinglong and other divine dragons, large and small, to the earth to control floods. When he arrived on the earth, he changed into a big, stout man, more than nine feet long, with a big nose, big eyes, a double layer of teeth in his mouth, and three holes in his ears.

Legend has it that the great flood on the earth was caused by the God of Water Gonggong's angry collision with Mount Buzhou. When Gongong heard that Yu was coming to control floods, he once again made waves and wanted to prevail over him from the very first encounter. Seeing that many people died in the flood, Yu became even more determined to control floods.

Before the work began, Yu held a meeting of the gods of the world at Mount Kuaiji to rally them to support his action of controlling floods and discuss the water treatment project together. At the meeting, a man called Fangfeng was not only late, but also had a negative attitude towards his action of controlling floods, spreading rumours that were not conducive to cooperative floods control, and he publicly executed Fangfeng.

The execution of Fangfeng demonstrated the determination to control floods, strict discipline and unity of thoughts, and cleared the way for him to control floods.

TIPS: The stories of Gun and Yu controlling floods are from the ancient book like *Shan Hai Jing*. Yu had the determination to control floods for the people, and even more determined action to achieve it. The fact that he paid attention to public opinions and mobilized the masses was one of the treasures of his success.

禹丈量九州

禹在着手治水前，一直在思考一个问题，那就是他父亲治水为何失败？于是他亲自到各地勘察灾情，沿着长江东下，又逆着黄河而上，走遍了济水、淮水等地，总结出父亲治水失败的原因：只一味采用筑堤的办法，用息壤修筑水堤坝，把洪水堵住；当堤坝里的水积多了，涨高了，堤坝便照样挡不住洪水，如果坝塌了，洪水更是瞬间变成了猛兽。

禹从父亲的教训中改变了治水战略，采用"以疏为主、以堵为辅"的方法，开山修渠，让洪水加快通过，合理分流。他让长有翅膀的应龙发挥其灵性，在前面考察，确定哪里适合开凿河流，传说我们今天所见的大江大河，都是那时大禹开凿的。同时，禹让那只对父亲忠心耿耿的大乌龟走在后面，把天帝赐给的息壤背在背上，随时拿息壤把那些有积水的深渊填平，把人类居住的地方加高。在那些需要特别加高的地方，禹便让那里有了大山。

禹始终牢记父亲的遗志，时时想着人民的苦难，十三年如一日，一心扑在治水上，几次经过家门都没有回家。他不仅是治水领导，而且处处亲力亲为，累得指甲磨秃了，小腿上的汗毛磨光了，半个身子不听使唤，走起路来也一瘸一拐，当时人们把他两只脚一前一后的步伐叫做"禹步"。

经过十几年的艰苦奋斗，禹终于治好了有名的大河三百条，支流小河三千条，更小的河流无数条。洪水平息了，大地上又长出一片新绿，老百姓回到家园安居乐业。

禹为弄清楚中国大地到底有多大，便命属神太章从东量到西，从北量到南，得出完全一样的数字，都是二亿三万三千五百里七十步，原来中华民族居住的地方，在禹的时代竟是方方正正的。禹为了更好地治理疆土，便把它划分为九州。

【阅读小贴士】失败是成功之母。善于总结经验，重视实地调研，尊重自然规律，把人民利益放在首位，这是禹治水成功的重要法宝。

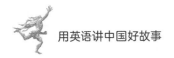

Yu Measuring His Country

Before he set out to control floods, Yu had been pondering the question of why his father had failed. So he went around the regions to survey the situation, going east along the Yangtze River and up the Yellow River, travelling all over the Ji and Huai Rivers, and concluded that the reason for his father's failure was that he had only used the method of building embankments with resting soil to stop the floods. When more water had accumulated in the dams and they rose, the dams could not stop the floods, and if the dams collapsed, the floods would instantly become fierce beasts.

Yu changed his water management strategy from his father's lesson and adopted the method of "**dredging** as the main method and blocking as the secondary method", opening mountains and building canals to speed up the passage of floodwaters and divert them rationally. He had the winged dragon, Yinglong, use his spiritual powers to scout ahead and determine which place to cut rivers, and legend has it that the great rivers we see today were all cut by Yu at that time. At the same time, he had the great tortoise, who was devoted to his father, walk behind him, carrying on his back the resting soil given by the Emperor of Heaven. He prepared it to margin the **abysses** where

dredge

v. 挖掘

abyss

n. 深渊

there was standing water and to raise the places where humans lived. In those places that needed special rising, he then made great mountains there.

Always mindful of his father's legacy and the suffering of the people, he devoted himself to floods controlling for thirteen years, passing through his home several times without returning. He was not only the leader of the water treatment, but also did everything by himself. He was so tired that these fingernails were bald, the sweat on his calves was worn out, half of his body was disobedient, and he walked with a limp, and people at that time called his two feet walking one behind the other Yu Step.

After more than ten years of hard work, he was able to heal the famous 300 large rivers, 3,000 small **tributaries** and countless smaller rivers. The floods subsided, the land grew green again, and the people returned to their homes to live and work in peace and happiness.

In order to find out how long and how wide the land was, he ordered the god Taizhang to measure from east to west and from north to south, and came up with the exact same figure of 230,300,500 miles and 70 paces, which turned out that the place Chinese people lived in was actually square in the time of Yu. In order to manage the territory better, he divided it into nine states.

TIPS: Failure is the mother of success. Learning from experience, researching in the field, respecting the laws of

tributary
n. 支流

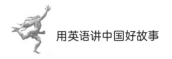

nature, and putting the interests of the people at first led to the success of Yu's flood controlling.

神话故事

"河图"和"玉简"的故事

治水是庞大的工程,禹成功治水,除了个人付出之外,也是集体力量的贡献。其中就流传着"河图"和"玉简"的故事。

这一天,禹站在黄河岸边观察水势,忽然从河中跳出来一个鱼身人面、自称是河神的神,他送给禹一块水淋淋的大青石板,转身便没入黄河中不见了。禹见青石板上面布满了线条形的花纹,再仔细一看,禹发现这是一幅治水的地图。此后禹便参照这青石板上的"河图"来劈山开路及疏导洪流。

在开凿龙门山的时候,禹又得到了另一样叫"玉简"的宝贝。

据说那时龙门山与吕梁山的山脉连在一起,是一座大山,位置在今天山西和陕西交界的地方,正好挡住了黄河的去路,河水到了这里流不过去,便形成倒流,连上游的龙门山都被淹没了。禹疏导黄河从青海的积石山来到这里,把龙门山一劈为二,使它分跨在黄河的东西两岸,像两扇门,让河水从峭壁的门户间奔腾而下,禹给这个地方取名为龙门。传说这里曾是江海中的大鲤鱼举行跳龙门比赛的地方,到了一定的时节,大鲤鱼们便汇集在此山崖下,举行跳龙门比赛,跳过去的就从此成龙升天了,跳不过去的仍回去做鱼儿。封建社会里把科举考试比喻为"鲤鱼跃龙门",考中了被喻为"登龙门",其说法即来源于此。

有一天,禹正领众神开凿龙门山,偶然进入一个大岩洞。洞里很深很黑,禹打起火把探路,走着走着,忽见前面有个东西闪闪发光,把整个岩洞照亮。禹仔细一看,发现是一条大黑蛇,嘴里衔着夜明珠,它在前面给禹带路。禹走到光明的地方,看见有一座殿堂,一个人面蛇身的大神坐在殿堂的中央,便上前问道:"您就是华胥氏的儿子伏羲吧?"

那蛇身人面的神正是伏羲,他对大禹说:"人间又闹洪水,老百姓无家可归,这是水神共工干的,我敬佩你的治水精神,在此等你,想助你一臂之

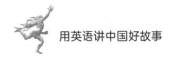

力。"说着从怀里掏出一支"玉简"交给禹,告诉禹可以用它来度量大地,平定水土。禹赶紧拜谢。

【阅读小贴士】禹治水是一项得民心的工程,不仅得到老百姓拥护,也得到神助。其实这里的"河图"和"玉简",都是中华民族集体智慧的结晶。

神话故事

Stories of River Map and Jade Tablet

Controlling floods was a huge project. The success of Yu's work was not only a matter of personal commitment but also of collective effort. The story of "river map" and "jade tablet" has been passed down to us.

On this day, Yu was standing on the bank of the Yellow River, observing the water, when suddenly a fish-bodied, human-faced god, claiming to be the river god, jumped out of the river, gave him a large, watery slab of green stone and disappeared after plunging into the Yellow River. He saw that the slab was covered with lines and patterns, and he took a closer look and realized that it was a map for water management. Thereafter, he referred to the "river map" on the slab to **cleave** mountains, build roads and divert floods.

cleave

v. 劈开, 砍开

During the excavation of Mount Longmen, he was given another treasure called "jade tablet".

It was said that at that time, Mount Longmen was a large mountain connected to the Lüliangs Mountains, located at the border of present-day Shanxi and Shaanxi, which blocked the path of the Yellow River. When the river could not flow through here, it backed up and flooded even Mount Longmen upstream. He came here from Mount

Jishi in Qinghai to channel the Yellow River, splitting the Mount Longmen in two so that it **straddled** the east and west banks of the Yellow River, like two gates, allowing the river to rush down between the **craggy** portals. He named this place the dragon gate. Legend has it that this was the place where the dragon gate jumping competition wes held for the big carp in the river and the sea. At a certain time of the year, the big carp gathered under this cliff and held the competition, and those who jumped over became dragons and ascended to heaven, and those who couldn't make the jump still went back to being fish. In feudal society, the imperial examination was likened to "the carp leaping from the dragon gate", and winning the examination was called "ascending to the dragon gate", which was the origin of the saying.

One day, when he was leading the gods to excavate Mount Longmen, he stumbled into a large rock cave. The cave was very deep and dark, so he started a torch to explore the way and as he walked, he suddenly saw something shining in front of him, illuminating the whole cave. When he looked carefully, he saw that it was a large black snake with a **luminous** pearl in its mouth, and it was leading the way for him. When he came to the place with light, he saw a hall in which a great god with a human face and snake body sat in the centre, he went up to him and asked, "You are Fuxi, the son of Huaxu, are you not?"

The snake-like, human-faced god was none other than Fuxi, and the god said to him, "There is another flood on

straddle

v. 跨坐；分腿站立

craggy

adj. 峻峭的

luminous

adj. 夜光的

the earth, and the people are homeless. This is the work belonging to the Water God Gonggong. I admire your spirit of floods controlling, and I'm here for you and want to help you!" Fuxi took a "jade tablet" out of his pocket and gave it to him, telling him that he could use it to measure the earth and calm the floods. He hurriedly thanked the god.

TIPS: Yu Controlling the Floods was a project that won the hearts of the people and was not only supported by the people but also helped by the god. In fact, the "river map" and the "jade tablet" are both the result of the collective wisdom of the Chinese people.

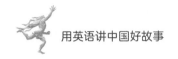

禹的婚事

禹一心扑在治理洪水上,把自己的婚事都给忘了,直到三十岁还没有结婚。

当他治水走到涂山(地名,也是氏族名)时,正好遇见当地有人迎娶新娘。禹突然意识到自己三十岁了,该结婚了!

有一天,禹看见一只有九条尾巴的白狐狸,向他跑来,一点也不害怕。当地传说,九尾白狐、龙、凤、麒麟都是吉祥动物。禹非常珍爱它,抚摸着它身上洁白而又漂亮的毛发,不禁想起涂山当地正流传的一首民谣,大意是说:谁见了九尾白狐,谁就可以当王;谁娶了涂山氏的女儿,谁就会家业兴旺。禹想,这白狐的出现和民谣的流传,也许就是他婚姻的征兆吧!

涂山当地有个美丽姑娘,名叫女娇,禹对她一见钟情,而女娇也早闻大禹是位治水的英雄,从心底里爱慕他。可是禹治水太忙,他略向姑娘表达心意后,又匆匆到南方治水了。女娇心中想念禹,却一直不见他归来,就随口唱了一首歌:"等候心上的人呀,日子过得多么慢啊!"据说这就是南国最早的情歌了。

有情人终成眷属。当禹从南方回来时,他和女娇举行了婚礼。可婚后第四天,禹又去远方治水了。

【阅读小贴士】禹因治水耽误了自己的婚事;成家后,又以自己承担的治水工作为重。这种牺牲精神,一直传颂至今,成为中华精神的一部分。

Marriage of Yu

Yu was so preoccupied with the control of floods that he forgot his marriage and did not marry until he was thirty.

When he came to Tushan (the name of a place and a clan), he met a local man who was marrying a bride. Suddenly he realized that he was thirty years old and should get married!

One day he saw a white fox with nine tails, running towards him, not afraid at all. Local legend has it that the nine-tailed white fox, the dragon, the phoenix and the unicorn are all auspicious animals. He cherished the fox very much and stroked its white and beautiful fur. He could not help but remember a local folk song that was being passed around in Tushan, to the effect that whoever saw the nine-tailed white fox would become king, and whoever married the daughter of the Tushan clan would have a prosperous family. He thought that the appearance of the white fox and the circulation of the ballad might be a sign of his marriage!

There was a beautiful local girl from Tushan named Nüjiao, and he fell in love with her at first sight. She had heard that Yu was a hero who controlled floods, and she loved him from the bottom of her heart. But he was

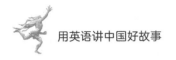

so busy that after expressing his feelings to the girl, he hurriedly went to the south to control floods. The girl missed him, but never saw him return. She sang a song casually, "How slowly the days pass, waiting for the one I love!" It was said to be the earliest love song in the south.

The lovers finally got married. When he returned from the south, they got married. But on the fourth day after the wedding, he went off to a faraway land to control floods again.

TIPS: Yu delayed his own marriage to control floods; and after he became a husband, he took on the work of floods control as his priority. The spirit of sacrifice, which has been celebrated to this day, has become part of the Chinese spirit.

神话故事

三过其门而不入

禹牢记父亲的遗志,全身心地投入治水的伟大事业中,顾不上自己的小家。在治水期间,禹曾三次经过家门口都没敢进去,流传着"三过其门而不入"的故事。

第一次经过家门时,禹的妻子女娇刚分娩不久,他站在屋外,听见婴儿哇哇啼哭声。他心情很激动,也很难过。助手劝他进屋去看看,他犹豫着,不敢轻易踏进屋内。因为他知道,此时治理洪水的事耽误不得。他也怕和妻子相见,彼此会更加难舍难分,不但不能安慰妻子,反而会带给妻子更多的烦恼和不安。于是他咬牙转身离去。

四年以后的一个中午,大禹第二次为治水经过家门口。他刚登上家门口不远的小丘,就看见坐在屋前的妻子,怀中搂着儿子在说笑。当妻子也看见他时,便立即起身抱起儿子,握着儿子的手冲他招手。他急切地朝妻儿走近,却被妻子泪流满面的笑容惊醒。他立马停住了脚步,又一次忍住内心的渴望,转身便要离去。妻子挽留他进家门歇息一会再走,他却说此时治水正是紧张时刻,嘱咐妻子在家等待他治水成功归来,便再次扭头离去。

禹第三次经过家门时,儿子已快十岁了,看到他就跑过来拉他回家。禹深情地抚摸着儿子的头,告诉他治水已经到了最后的关键时刻,他必须抓紧时间,尽快做好治水工程的收尾工作,不能因疏忽大意而出一点差错。妻子也过来掰开儿子的手说:"等你爹爹平息了洪水就回家,回家后他就再也不离开我们了。"禹听后非常感动,更坚定了早日治好洪水的决心,便立刻转身上路了。尽管他很想再多看妻儿一眼,很想进屋喝口水再走,但他仍是摇着头,匆匆离去。

【阅读小贴士】禹治水"三过家门而不入"的故事众所周知,这种大公无私的精神,受到了百姓的赞扬,也为舜帝所器重,所以舜晚年才放心地把帝位禅让给了禹。后来,人们用"三过家门而不入"来表达舍小家为大家的牺牲精神。

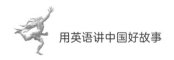

Yu Passing by His House Three Times Without Entering

Remembering his father's legacy, Yu devoted himself to the great cause of controlling floods, having no time to care about his own family. It was said that during the period of floods control, Yu passed by his own door three times without daring to step in, and the story goes that "Yu Passing by his house three times without entering".

The first time he passed by, his wife had just given birth and he stood outside the house. When he heard the baby crying, he was very excited and sad. As his helpers urged him to go in and take a look, he hesitated and was afraid to step inside. He knew that floods control could not be delayed at this time. He was afraid that if he met his wife, they would be even more inseparable, and instead of comforting her, he would bring her more trouble and anxiety. Therefore, he **gritted** his teeth and turned away.

One noon, four years later, he passed by his house for the second time in order to control floods. He had just climbed the hill not far from his home when he saw his wife sitting in front of the house, laughing and talking with their son in her arms. When his wife also saw him, she immediately got up and picked up her son, holding the son's hand and waving at him. He approached his wife and

grit

v. 咬紧牙关

son eagerly, but was startled by his wife's tearful smile. He immediately stopped walking, held back his inner longing once again and turned to leave. His wife asked him to come home and rest for a while before leaving, but he said that it was a tense time for floods control. He told her to wait at home for his successful return and then turned away.

The third time he passed by his house, his son, who was almost ten years old, ran to pull him home. He stroked his son's head affectionately and told him that the floods control has in the final critical situation and he must hurry up to finish the final work as soon as possible. He must not make any mistakes because of carelessness. His wife also came over and broke his son's hand, saying, "When your father calms the flood, he will go home, and when he gets home, he will never leave us." Hearing these words, he was so moved that he was determined to finish the work of controlling floods as soon as possible. So he immediately turned around and went on his way. Although he wanted to see his wife and son one more time and to go inside for a drink of water before leaving, he shook his head and left in a hurry.

TIPS: The story of Yu who passed by his house three times without entering is well known. His selfless spirit was praised by the people and valued by Emperor Shun, so Shun was relieved to give the throne to Yu in his later years. Later on, people used the story to express the spirit of sacrificing individual interests to protect public benefits.

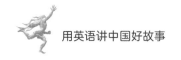

启母石的传说

关于禹与妻子女娇的婚后生活，还有另外一种传说和记载：禹婚后曾经带着妻子一起，前往轩辕山治水。此山险峻，只有打通它，洪水才能往下流。

禹对妻子女娇说："开通这山不容易，我得努力奋战。我在山崖边上挂着一面鼓。等我干活饿了，就去击鼓，你听见鼓响，再做饭给我送过来。"妻子说："好。"此后，两人就以击鼓为号，表明吃饭的时间到了。

一天，为了加快挖山的速度，禹化作一头力大无比的黑熊，连推带挖，效率提高好几倍。在他干得起劲的时候，山上滚落一块石头，正好砸在山崖边的皮鼓上。女娇听到鼓声，心想丈夫干活饿了，便赶忙烧火做饭，带着怀孕的身体，爬上山给禹送饭。当她到达时，没看到丈夫的身影，只看到一头大黑熊正在拱着大山，女娇吓得大叫一声，丢下饭篮子，扭头就跑。

禹听到了妻子的惊叫声，回过头来，看到妻子吓得跑远，他也慌了，赶忙奔向妻子，想向她解释一下。可因为事发突然，禹忘记把自己变回人形。妻子回头看见大黑熊朝自己追过来，惊恐不已，竟化作了一块巨石。

禹看到之后非常伤心，后悔没有将自己能变成黑熊的事告诉妻子。他大声呼唤着妻子，可是女娇再也变不回来了。最后，禹对着巨石大喊："还我的孩子！"话音刚落，只听一声巨响，巨石裂开了，从中蹦出的一个婴儿，这便是禹的儿子启。"启"就是"裂开"的意思。这个石头里生出的孩子非常不一般，他后来继承了禹的帝王之位，成为夏朝的开国君主。

后来，人们就把女娇变成的那块石头叫做"启母石"。

【阅读小贴士】这篇神话故事，颂扬了禹一家为治水做出的牺牲，表达的是人们对治水英雄禹的敬爱与美好愿望。

Legend of Stone Memorializing Qi's Mother

There is another legend and account of the married life of Yu and his wife Nüjiao: Yu took his wife to go to Mount Xuanyuan to control floods. This mountain was so **treacherous** that the only way for the floods to flow down was to break it.

treacherous
adj. 险峻

He said to his wife Nüjiao, "Opening this mountain is not easy, and I have to fight hard. I have a drum hanging on the edge of the cliff. When I get hungry from my work, I will beat the drum, and when you hear the drum, you can cook and bring me food." The wife agreed with what he said. After the words, the two of them used the beating of the drum as a signal that it was a time to eat.

One day, in order to speed up the digging of the mountain, he took the form of a black bear with immense strength. The efficiency was increased greatly by pushing and digging together. While he was working hard, a stone rolled down the hill and hit a leather drum on the edge of the cliff. When his wife heard the drums, she thought that her husband was hungry for work, so she rushed to cook with her pregnant body, climbed up the mountain to bring her husband food. When she arrived at the place where her husband had been working, she didn't see him but found

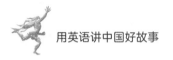

a large black bear arching over the mountain. She shouted in fear, dropped the rice basket, turned her head and ran away.

He heard his wife's **shriek** and looked back, seeing his wife running away in fear. He also panicked and rushed to her, trying to explain the situation to her. But he had forgotten to change himself back into his original form because of the suddenness of the incident. When his wife turned around and saw the big black bear coming after her, she was so terrified that she turned into a huge stone.

shriek
v. 尖叫

He was devastated when he saw this situation and regretted not telling his wife that he could turn into a black bear. He called out to his wife, but she could never change back. Finally, he shouted at the stone, "Give back my child!" As soon as the words left his mouth, there was a loud bang and the stone split open and a baby appeared, who was his son Qi. The word "Qi" means "split open". The child born from the stone was so extraordinary that he succeeded Yu as the emperor and became the founder of the Xia Dynasty.

Later on, people called the stone into which Nüjiao had been transformed "the Stone Memorializing Qi's Mother".

TIPS: This mythical tale celebrates the sacrifices made by the family of Yu to control floods, and expresses people's respect and good wishes for the flood-controlling hero Yu.

三门峡的由来

黄河上的璀璨明珠三门峡,相传也是禹治水时开辟出来的。

当年禹治水来到这里,发现有座名叫砥柱山的大山阻碍了黄河去路,便挥动神斧,朝着阻隔黄河水的砥柱山劈去,最终把砥柱山劈成了三道峡谷,犹如三道门,将黄河之水在此分流。

当黄河之水奔腾而来时,三道峡谷在此又呈现出各自不同的风采。人们便根据每道峡谷的特点,形象地把三道峡谷比作三道门,并称之为"人门、神门、鬼门",三门峡之名由此而来。从此,黄河之水沿黄土高原一路高歌,自北向南顺流抵达秦岭,然后将三门峡环抱其中;又因这里河道狭窄,水流湍急,形成"四面环山三面水"美景,而后拐弯东去,非常壮观。

今天"三门天险"已经没有了,取而代之的是一条横贯峡谷的大坝,像一条银色的缎带把山西、河南两省连接起来,这就是黄河第一坝——三门峡水利枢纽工程。随着三门峡大坝建设而崛起的一座新兴旅游城市就是今天的河南省三门峡市。在这里,至今还留有当年禹治水的遗迹。

【阅读小贴士】禹治水时以疏导为重要原则,逢山开山,遇洼筑堤,疏通水道,引洪水入海。人们将自然界鬼斧神工形成的峡谷奇观三门峡,想象为禹所为,其实是对禹治水功绩的颂扬。如今,在黄河的中流矗立着一根像大柱子似的山石,称为"砥柱",传说是禹开采"砥柱山"时留下的。"中流砥柱"这个成语也由此而来,称赞那些在风险面前意志坚定、毫不动摇的人,而禹便是最好的写照。

Origin of Sanmen Xia

Sanmen Xia (Three Gates Gorge), a bright pearl on the Yellow River, is also said to have been cleaved by Yu when he was controlling floods.

When Yu came to this area to control floods over 5,000 years ago, he found a mountain named Dizhu like a death gorge blocking the Yellow River, so he swung his divine axe towards it and split it into three pieces, like three gates, to divert the water from the Yellow River.

When the water of the Yellow River rushes in, the three gorges take on different appearances. Based on the characteristics of each gorge, people imagined that the three gorges were three gates, and called them the Gate of Man (Ren Men), the Gate of God (Shen Men) and the Gate of Ghost (Gui Men)—hence came the name Sanmen Xia (Three Gates Gorge). As the name suggests, one can imagine the meaning of each gorge from the names of the three gates. Since then, the water of the Yellow River has flowed downstream along the **Loess Plateau** from north to south to Qinling Mountains, and then encircling the gorges. The river way is narrow and the current is fast, forming beautiful scenery of "mountains on four sides and water on three sides", and then it turns to the east, which is very spectacular.

Losess Plateau	黄土高原

Today, the three gates of natural barriers are gone, replaced by a dam that runs across the canyon, connecting Shanxi and Henan provinces like a silver ribbon. That is the first dam of Yellow River—Sanmenxia Water Control Project. With the establishment of the first Yellow River dam, Sanmenxia City was built up as a newly industrial and tourist city in central China's Henan Province. Today there are still relics of the time when Yu controlled floods in the region.

TIPS: When Yu controlled floods, he used dredging as an important principle, cleaving mountains and building dams in depressions to dredge waterways and divert floodwaters into the sea. People imagine that the canyon wonders formed by nature's magic craftsmanship are the work of Yu, which is actually a celebration of his contributions to controlling floods. Nowadays, in the middle stream of the Yellow River stands a big pillar-like stone called Dizhu, which is said to be left by Yu when he mined Mount Dizhu. The idiom "mainstay of the middle stream" is also derived from this legend, praising those who are determined and unwavering in the face of risks, and Yu is the best depiction of this idiom.

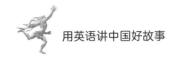

禹治淮河

禹成功开凿三门峡后,继续沿着黄河水流梳理河道,来到离三门峡不远的桐柏山。

桐柏山是淮河的源头,淮河经常泛滥成灾,给沿岸百姓带来灾难,禹多次来这里治水,都不是很成功。当禹再次启动治水工程时,看到了一种奇怪现象:河水翻腾,风雷齐作,天昏地暗,鬼哭狼嚎。民间有谣言四起,说是有妖精作怪,搞得人心惶惶,治水工程无法进行下去。

禹知道人们的担忧,召集各路神仙开会,商讨降妖办法。有四个山神态度消极,害怕妖怪的威力,也怀疑禹治妖的决心,给禹治水带来很大阻力。禹果断地将四位山神囚禁起来,不让他们妖言惑众,动摇众心,同时抓紧部署降妖工作。

原来传说中的水妖名叫无支祁,长得像猿猴,塌鼻子,凸额头,白头青身,火眼金睛。它的头颈长达百尺,力气超过九头大象,而身子却灵活得像只猴,可以跃入天空,转眼又可潜入河底,的确本领高强,神通广大。它常在淮河一带兴风作浪,危害百姓。周边人早对它闻风丧胆,怕得要命。

禹组织众神了解无支祁的情况,分析它的特点,寻找它的弱点,制定降妖的策略,终于通过多轮激战,无支祁中箭受伤被擒,禹用大铁索锁住了它的颈脖,拿金铃穿在它的鼻子上,把它压在淮阴龟山脚下,从此淮河才得以平静地流入东海。

【阅读小贴士】据记载,淮河水怪无支祁是尧舜禹时期出现的奇妖,出生在豫南桐柏山脉中的花果山,为天生神猴。其形象第一次出现在北宋《太平广记》中,今推测为孙悟空原型。

Yu Harnessing Huai River

After successfully excavating Sanmen Xia, Yu continued to comb the river ways along the Yellow River, coming to Mount Tongbai, not far from the gorges.

Tongbai was the source of the Huai River, which often flooded and caused disasters for the people along its banks, so Yu came here several times to control floods, but having no success. When he started the floods-controlling project again, he saw a strange phenomenon: the river was tossing, the wind was blowing, the thunder was **grumbling**, the sky was murky, the earth was dark and ghosts were crying. Rumours spread among the people that there were demons appearing, making people fearful and it impossible to carry out the project.

grumble
v. 咕哝

Knowing the concerns of the people, Yu had a meeting gathering different gods to discuss ways to subdue the demons. Four mountain gods had negative attitudes; they feared the power of the demons and doubted Yu's determination to punish them, causing much resistance to his floods control. He decisively imprisoned the four mountain gods to prevent them from confusing the public with their demonic words and shaking the hearts of the people. At the same time, he hurried to assign the work of subduing the demons.

It turned out that legendary water demon was named Wuzhiqi, which looked like an ape with a collapsed nose, a convex forehead, a white head, a green body, and golden eyes. His head and neck are hundred feet long, and his strength exceeds that of nine elephants, while his body is as nimble as a monkey's. It could leap into the sky and dive to the bottom of the river in a short time, so it was indeed a powerful and magical creature. It was often found making waves around Huai Rver, causing harm to the people. The people around were already very afraid of it.

Yu organized the gods to find more information about Wuzhiqi, analyzed its characteristics, searched for its weaknesses and devised a strategy to subdue it. Finally, after many rounds of fierce battles, the monster in Huai River was captured with an arrow and wounded. He locked its neck with a large iron rope, put a golden bell through its nose and pinned it down at the foot of Mount Gui in Huaiyin. Only then did the Huai River flow calmly into the East China Sea.

TIPS: According to the records, the water monster Wuzhiqi in Huai River was a strange demon that appeared during the time of Yao, Shun and Yu. It was born in Mount Huaguo of Tongbai Mountains in southern Henan, which was born as a divine monkey. Its image first appeared in *Taiping Guangji* in the Northern Song Dynasty, and is now presumed to be the prototype of Sun Wukong.

禹铸九鼎

禹治水十三年，兴修水利，有效解决了中原洪水泛滥成灾的问题，让老百姓过上了安稳日子，万民敬仰，称他为"大禹"，即"伟大的禹"。

帝舜在位三十三年时，正式把天子之位禅让给禹。禹继位后，先后对赋税等方面的事务进行了整治规范，经济社会发展繁荣稳定，国家和百姓日益富庶，呈现出了万国遵从、九州稳定、四海升平的盛世景象。

禹即位第四年，大臣向禹请示道："现在九州所贡之金年年积多，作何用处呢？"禹想起从前轩辕黄帝功成铸鼎，鼎成仙去，打算铸造九鼎，以示天下太平。

九州指冀州、兖州、青州、徐州、扬州、荆州、豫州、梁州和雍州。以一鼎象征一州，每个宝鼎分别由各州用其所献贡金自行铸造，并刻绘本州的珍禽异兽和鬼魅精怪的图像。禹铸鼎要让天下百姓从宝鼎上去了解自己身边及各地都有什么精怪及它们长什么样。在以后出行时，可提前做好防范准备，备好降妖或制服对方的工具，以保生命安全。

传说到了春秋时候，楚庄王带兵攻打陆浑戎（小国名），走到周天子的都城洛邑（今河南洛阳），周定王派使臣王孙满接待他。筵席上，楚庄王向王孙满问起九鼎，颇有取周朝而代之的意思。善于外交辞令的王孙满说了一句讽刺他的话："在德不在鼎。"意思是说，国君统治天下在于有德，而不在于是否有鼎，这让楚庄王碰了一鼻子灰。后来，世人把这件事称为"楚庄王问鼎"或"问鼎中原"，成了一句野心家要夺取帝王之位的代名词。

【阅读小贴士】禹铸九鼎，既是纪念治水成功，也是向百姓普及生存知识。"九鼎"代表华夏九州，后来逐渐演变为国家统一和王权的象征。

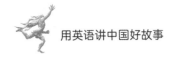

Yu Casting Nine Tripods

For thirteen years, Yu controlled floods and built water conservancy projects that effectively solved the problem of flooding in the central plains, allowing the people to live in peace and security. He was revered by all the people and called "Da Yu", or "Yu the Great".

When Emperor Shun reigned for thirty-three years, he formally ceded the throne to Yu. After he succeeded to the throne, he successively regulated taxation and other matters, and the economic and social development became prosperous and stable, the country and the people became more and more **affluent**, presenting a prosperous scene in which all the nations obeyed, the whole country of nine provinces was stable and the four seas were at peace.

In the fourth year of Yu's reign, the minister asked the emperor, "What's the use of the gold from the nine provinces, which is now accumulated year by year?" He remembered that once upon a time Emperor Xuanyuan had finished his work and cast the tripod, and when the tripod became immortal, he intended to cast nine tripods(Jiuding) as a sign of peace in the world.

The nine provinces of China were Jizhou, Yanzhou, Qingzhou, Xuzhou, Yangzhou, Jingzhou, Yuzhou, Liangzhou and Yongzhou. Each tripod, standing for a

affluent

adj. 富裕的

province, was cast by each state with its own tribute gold, and was engraved with descriptions of the region's rare animals, ghosts, monsters and spirits. The purpose of casting the tripods was to let the people of the world know from the tripods what spirits and monsters were around and what they looked like. When they travelled in the future, they could be prepared in advance and have tools to subdue them in order to keep their lives safe.

Legend has it that during the Spring and Autumn Period, King Zhuang of Chu led his troops to attack Lu Hunrong (the name of a small country) and came to Luo Yi (now Luoyang, Henan), the capital of Emperor Zhou, where King Ding of Zhou sent his envoy Wang Sunman to receive him. At the banquet, King Zhuang of Chu asked Wang Sunman about the nine tripods, with the intention of taking over the Zhou dynasty. Wang Sunman, who was good at diplomatic rhetoric, made a **sarcastic** remark on him, "It is in the virtue but not in the tripods." This meant that the emperor rules the country depending on his virtue, not on whether or not he has a tripod, and this answer made the king embarrassed. Later, this incident became known as "King Zhuang of Chu asked for the tripod" or "asking for the tripod in the central plains", which became a synonym for ambitious people who wanted to seize the throne of the emperor.

TIPS: Yu Casting Nine Tripods commemorates the success of his floods control and spreads the knowledge of survival to

sarcastic

adj. 讽刺的；嘲讽的

the people. These gaint bronze cauldrons represent the nine provinces of China, and later have evolved into a symbol of the unity of the country and the supremacy of kingship.

神话故事

哪吒闹海

传说哪吒出生时,是一个肉球。他的父亲托塔李天王李靖以为是不祥之物,于是一剑劈开,结果从里面蹦出一个俊俏的男孩,这就是后来的神童哪吒。

哪吒刚出生就会说话、会走路,嘴里还能喷火,吓得李靖又要拔剑劈去,谁知小男孩边跑向母亲求救,边质问李靖:"爹,你为什么要杀我?"

就在李靖不知所措时,一位白胡子老人推门进来,自称是乾元山金光洞太乙真人,要收小男孩为徒,为他取名哪吒。离开前,他还从怀里掏出两件宝物送给小徒弟,就是神童哪吒从小把玩的武器乾坤圈和混天绫。

哪吒自幼喜欢习武,三岁的一天,他同小伙伴在海边嬉戏,正好碰上巡海夜叉与东海龙王三太子敖丙出来肆虐百姓,残害儿童。小哪吒见此恶徒,义愤填膺,挺身而出,打死夜叉与三太子又抽了它的龙筋。

东海龙王得知儿子被小哪吒打死,勃然大怒。他请来西海、南海及北海龙王一起降罪于哪吒的父亲,兴风作浪,口吐洪水淹没陈塘关。小哪吒知道自己惹祸了,便站出来对东海龙王说:"打死你儿子的人是我,要报仇找我!我可以死,但你必须放过我父母及本城的老百姓。"说罢,小哪吒抽剑自刎。龙王看哪吒已死,这才罢休离去。

就在哪吒父母伤心哭泣之时,哪吒的师父太乙真人骑着白鹤从天而降,借着荷叶莲花之气,让哪吒脱胎换骨,从此有了莲花不死之身,跟随师父继续学习本领。后来,哪吒大闹东海,砸了龙宫,捉了龙王,为民除害。哪吒多次降魔有功,被玉帝和如来加封神位,统领天兵神将,镇压天下妖孽,成为善与美的化身。

【阅读小贴士】哪吒相传为孩童天神,元代神话典籍《三教搜神大全》中就有记载,是天上人间公认的少年小英雄,也是古代文学形象中少有的儿童形象,被历代儿童读者所喜爱。

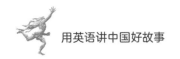

Nezha Conquering the Sea

Legend has it that when Nezha was born, he was a ball of flesh. His father, a millitary commander named Li Jing, thought it was an **ominous** object and attacked it with his sword, only to find a handsome boy came out of it, later known as the **prodigy** Nezha.

ominous
adj. 不祥的

prodigy
n. 神童

He was born talking, walking, and spitting fire from his mouth, so Li Jing was scared to draw his sword again, but the little boy ran to his mother for help while questioning his father, "Dad, why do you want to kill me?"

Just as his father was at a loss for words, an old man with a white beard pushed the door open and came in, claiming to be Taiyi Immortal of the Golden Light Cave on Mount Qianyuan. He offered to take the young boy as his pupil and named him Nezha. Before he left, he took out two treasures from his arms and gave them to his young pupil. The two treasures were Qiankun Circle(universe bracelet) and the magic Huntian Aya, both of which became body protection as well as weapons of the prodigy Nezha.

He had been fond of martial arts since he was a child. One day, when he was three years old, he was playing with his friends on the beach when they came across the nightstick and the third prince Ao Bing of the Dragon King of the East China Sea, who had come out to harm people and kill children. He was outraged by this villain and put himself forward, killing the nightstick and the third prince, and pulling the prince's keels.

The Dragon King of the East China Sea was furious when he learned that his son had been killed by Nezha. He invited the Dragon Kings of the West Sea, South Sea and North Sea to join him in smiting Nezha's father, making waves and flooding the Chentang Pass. Nezha knew that he had made trouble, so he stood up to the Dragon King and said, "I am the one who killed your son. If you want to revenge, call me! I can die, but you must spare my parents and the people of this city." After saying the words, he drew his sword and killed himself. The Dragon King saw that he was dead, so he stopped and left.

Just as his parents were weeping with sadness, his master Taiyi Immortal came down from the sky on a white crane. The master relied on the energy of the lotus leaf and the lotus flower to make Nezha reshape his body and from then on he has the immortal body of the lotus, and then his pupil could follow him to continue learning the skills. Later, Nezha conquered the East China Sea, smashing the Dragon Palace and capturing the Dragon King to eliminate evil for the people. After many successful attempts to subdue the demons, he was **canonized** by the Jade Emperor and Buddha and became the embodiment of goodness and beauty as he took command of the heavenly army and suppressed the demons of the world.

canonize

v. 宣圣

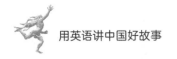 用英语讲中国好故事

TIPS: Nezha is a legendary Child-god of Heaven and was recorded in the Yuan Dynasty mythology book *Sanjiao Soushen Daquan*. He is recognized as a young hero of the world, and is also one of the rare children's images in ancient literature, loved by children readers for generations.

宝莲灯传奇

相传，很久很久之前，女娲娘娘有盏非常漂亮的神灯。这盏神灯从外形上看很像一朵刚刚绽放的莲花，通体透亮，光芒四射，因此女娲娘娘为它取名宝莲灯。后来，女娲娘娘将它作为生日贺礼送给了王母娘娘，王母娘娘又将它赠送给了仙女三圣母，即华山圣母。

三圣母长大后，天庭派她去统辖华山。三圣母带着宝莲灯到了华山，将华山一带治理得风调雨顺，老百姓过上了平安快乐的日子，都对她十分敬重。

这一天，赴京赶考的书生刘彦昌经过华山，遭遇了狂风暴雨，他身体虚弱，加上一路舟车劳顿，昏倒了。好心的三圣母在巡山时发现了他，将他救回。刘彦昌醒后，对美丽善良的三圣母产生了好感，三圣母也逐渐喜欢上了刘彦昌。没过多久，两人结为夫妻。

转眼间，秋天到了，刘彦昌要进京考试。这时三圣母已经怀孕了，刘彦昌临走时把一块祖传的沉香交给三圣母，叮嘱说生了孩子就叫沉香。刘彦昌走了没多久，小沉香就出生了。

不久，三圣母的哥哥二郎神听说妹妹嫁给了凡人，还生了个孩子，特别恼火，立刻带领天兵天将到华山兴师问罪。三圣母觉得自己没有错，不想回天庭。她被迫举起宝莲灯来护身，宝莲灯放射出万道五彩光芒，这些五彩灯光迅速地旋转起来，最后化作了一道极具威力的雷，将二郎神击倒在地。吃了败仗的二郎神跌坐在地上，领教了宝莲灯的威力。随后他心生一计，将哮天犬叫来，悄悄地在它耳边嘱咐了几句……

二郎神再次跑来向三圣母挑战，哮天犬趁机偷偷溜进屋里，叼走了还是婴儿的沉香，又故意从三圣母身旁经过。三圣母见自己的儿子被哮天犬叼走了，马上追赶过去，就在三圣母一心想着救下儿子时，哮天犬突然放下沉香，一口叼走了宝莲灯。

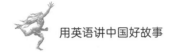

二郎神抢到了宝莲灯,轻松打败了三圣母,把她带回了天庭受罚。天庭命二郎神将三圣母带回华山,将她压在莲花峰下的黑云洞里。狠心的二郎神还想把沉香扔到山谷里,幸好霹雳大仙路过山谷,救了沉香。霹雳大仙把沉香带回自己住的仙人峰,教他本领。

话说刘彦昌进京赶考,中了状元,皇上封他做了大官。宰相一看刘彦昌前途无量,就想把自己的女儿嫁给刘彦昌,但被刘彦昌拒绝了。宰相失了颜面,怀恨在心,派人追杀刘彦昌,他一路逃难,刚巧也被霹雳大仙救下,送回了华山。刘彦昌在华山上找不到三圣母,伤心极了,就在山脚下住下来,等待三圣母的归来。

【阅读小贴士】宝莲灯是古代神话中最早出现的宝物,因为它是女娲娘娘送给王母娘娘的生日礼物,有着无边的法力,是三圣母的护身符。围绕宝莲灯的得失,演绎了一个沉香救母的感人故事。

Legend of Lotus Lantern

According to legend, long time ago, the goddess Nüwa had a very beautiful divine lantern. The lantern looked like a lotus flower that had just blossomed; it was so bright and radiant that she named it the magic lotus lantern. Later, she gave it to Queen Mother as a birthday gift, who in turn gave it to the fairy Sanshengmu, also known as Saint Mother on Mount Hua.

Sanshengmu was sent to take charge of Mount Hua When she grew up. After she arrived there with the magic lotus lantern, she governed the area of Mount Hua with good weather and the people respected her as they were able to live in peace and happiness.

One day, Liu Yanchang, a **mortal** scholar going to the capital city for his exams, passed by Mount Hua and was caught in a violent wind storm. He was weak and fainted because of the tiring journey. The kind-hearted Sanshengmu found him on her tour of the mountain and rescued him. After the scholar woke up, he took a liking to the beautiful and kind godness, who also gradually fell in love with him. It was not long before the two got married.

In a twinkling, it was autumn and Liu Yanchang wanted to take the imperial exam in the capital city. By this time his wife was pregnant. When he was

mortal

adj. 凡人的

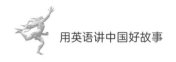

about to leave, he gave the wife an ancestral piece of eaglewood(chenxiang) and told her that their child would be named "Chenxiang". Not long after he left, the little baby was born.

Soon, Sanshengmu's brother, God Erlang, heard that his younger sister had married a mortal and had a child. Furiously, he came to Mount Hua to denouce her with the heavenly soldiers. But Sanshengmu didn't want to go back to Heaven. The godness was forced to hold up the lotus lantern to protect herself, which radiated thousands of multicoloured lights that spun rapidly and finally turned into a very powerful thunderbolt that knocked her brother to the ground. The defeated God Erlang fell to the ground and experienced the power of the lotus lantern. Then he had a plan. He called his faithful dog Howling Celestial Dog, quietly whispered a few instructions in its ear...

God Erlang came again to challenge his sister; the dog took the opportunity to sneak into the house, carried the baby Chenxiang off, and deliberately passed by Sanshengmu. The mother saw her son was gripped by the dog, immediately chased over, when she was thinking of saving her son, the dog suddenly put down the baby and gripped away the lotus lantern.

God Erlang snatched the lotus lantern, easily defeated the godness and brought her back to the Heaven to be punished. He then imprisoned his sister in a dark cave under the Lotus Peak of Mount Hua. The ruthless God Erlang also wanted to throw Chenxiang into a valley, but fortunately the God of Thunder passed by the valley and saved him. The god took him back to the immortal peak where he lived and taught him skills.

It was said that Liu Yanchang did well in the exam in the capital city and became the champion scholar; he was appointed a senior official. When the prime minister saw that he had a great future, he wanted to marry his daughter to Liu Yanchang, but the latter refused. The prime minister lost face and was so angry that he sent people after him. He fled all the way and happened to be saved by the God of Thunder and sent back to Mount Hua. He could not find Sanshengmu on Mount Hua and was so sad that he stayed at the foot of the mountain, waiting for the return of his wife.

TIPS: The magic lotus lantern is the earliest treasure to appear in ancient mythology, as it was a birthday gift from Nüwa to the Queen Mother with boundless magical power and a talisman for Sanshengmu. Around the gain or loss of the lotus lantern, a touching story of "Chenxiang Saving His Mother" is performed.

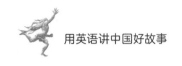

沉香救母

转眼间,十六年过去了,沉香长成了帅小伙,跟随霹雳大仙学了一身本领,还会七十三变。霹雳大仙看到沉香武艺学成了,就把他的身世告诉了他。沉香一听,急得立刻就要拜别师父,去救母亲。

霹雳大仙说:"别着急,孩子。你得先找到宝莲灯,再找到神斧,这样才能劈开华山,救出你的母亲。"

"宝莲灯在哪里?神斧又在哪里?"沉香急切地问。

"宝莲灯是你母亲的宝物,现在被藏在二郎神的真君庙里,你要想办法拿出宝莲灯,然后再去昆仑山找神斧。"

"为什么不让我直接去找神斧呢?"

"那可是当年盘古开天地的神斧,有三位非常厉害的天神看守着呢。"霹雳大仙说,"这三位天神都有很强的法力,你必须有宝莲灯的帮助才能拿到神斧。"

"知道了师父。"沉香说完就出发了。

沉香在二郎神的真君庙里找到了宝莲灯,刚把宝莲灯藏进怀里,就被二郎神发现了,两人展开恶斗,几个回合下来,沉香不是二郎神的对手,就在落败之际,忽然怀里的宝莲灯发出强烈的光芒,把二郎神弹开,向远处飞去。

沉香得到了宝莲灯,又向昆仑山出发。昆仑山上有一座寒冰洞,洞里是千年不化的寒冰,那把威力无比的神斧就藏在寒冰洞中。可是,从来没有人能从寒冰洞中活着走出去。沉香勇敢地走进了寒冰洞,那些冒着凉气的寒冰,似乎吸走了沉香全身的热气,沉香觉得自己快被冻僵了。

"放弃吧,孩子。"看守神斧的天神说。

"不,我一定要救母亲出来!"沉香坚定地说。

沉香的孝心感动了冰神、权神和死神三位天神,他们也抵挡不住宝莲灯

的威力,就让沉香取走了神斧。

沉香扛着神斧来到华山,举起神斧就向华山山峰砍去,就听"轰隆隆"一声,山峰一下子就从中间被劈开了,三圣母从山下飞了出来。

"娘!"沉香终于看到了自己的母亲。

"娘子!"刘彦昌终于等到了三圣母。

沉香劈山救母的孝心和勇气打动了玉皇大帝,他将三圣母的罪行赦免,并准许她跟刘彦昌生活在一起。沉香也被封为了神仙,一家人从此团圆了。

传说,沉香劈山时脚下所踩的那块土地上,长出了一座小山峰,当地老百姓称它为"孝子峰"。据说,人们登上孝子峰峰顶的时候,还能听到当年沉香大声呼叫母亲的声音。

【阅读小贴士】沉香救母的故事,兼具神话和童话的魅力,充满传奇和正能量,是一首真善美的赞歌。故事被改编为动画片和电视剧的《宝莲灯》,成为中华文化的生动形象,在海内外有着广泛的影响力。

Chenxiang Saving His Mother

In a twinkling, 16 years had passed and Chenxiang had grown up to be a handsome young man who had learned many skills from the God of Thunder and could change into 73 forms. When the god saw that Chenxiang had completed his martial arts skills, he told him about his origins. When Chenxiang heard the words, he was so anxious to bid farewell to his master and go to save his mother. The god said, "Don't worry, child. You have to find the lotus lantern first and then the divine axe so that you can split Mount Hua and save your mother."

"Where is the lotus lantern? And where is the divine axe?" Chenxiang asked eagerly.

"The lotus lantern is your mother's treasure and is now hidden in God Erlang's Temple of the True God, so you need to think of a way to get out the lantern and then go to Mount Kunlun to find the divine axe."

"Why don't you let me go directly to find the divine axe?"

"It is the divine axe that Pan Gu used to create the heaven and the earth, and it is guarded by three powerful heavenly gods." The god said, "These three heavenly gods all have very strong magic power, and you must get the help of the lotus lantern to get the divine axe."

"I understood, master." He said and set off.

He found the lotus lantern in God Erlang's Temple, and was found when he began to hide the lantern in his arms. They began a vicious fight, after a few rounds, he was not God Erlang's opponent. On the verge of defeat, suddenly the lotus lantern in his arms **emitted** a strong light; God Erlang was bounced away and flew away into the distance.

Chenxiang got the lantern back and set off for Mount Kunlun again. There was a cold ice cave on the mountain, which was full of cold ice that would not melt for thousand years, and the powerful axe was hidden in the cave. However, no one had ever been able to walk out of the cave alive. He entered the cave bravely. The cold ice with cold air seemed to suck the heat out of his body and he felt like he was freezing.

"Give up, child," said the heavenly god who guarded the divine axe.

"No, I must save my mother out!" He said firmly.

His piety touched the three heavenly gods, namely the God of Ice, the God of Power and the God of Death, and they also could not resist the power of the lotus lantern and let him take the divine axe.

He carried the divine axe to Mount Hua and raised it to cleave the peak of the mountain, and heard a "rumble", the middle part of the mountain peak was split down at once, and his mother Sanshengmu flew out from under the mountain.

emit

v. 发出；散发

"Mother!" Chenxiang finally saw his mother.

"Dear!" Liu Yanchang finally saw his wife.

Chenxiang's filial piety and courage in splitting the mountain to save his mother moved the Jade Emperor, who pardoned Sanshengmu for her crimes and allowed her to live with Liu Yanchang. Chenxiang was made a god and the family was reunited from then on.

Legend has it that a small peak grew out of the land on which Chenxiang stepped when he cleaved the mountain, and the local people called it the "Xiaozi Peak" (peak of a son who shows filial piety). It was said that when people climb to the top of the peak, they can still hear the voice of Chenxiang calling out to his mother.

TIPS: The legendary story of "Chenxiang Saving His Mother" both has a charm of myth and fairy tale, full of legends and positive energy. It's a hymn to truth, goodness and beauty. "The Magic Lotus Lantern" has been adapted into an animated film and a TV series, becoming a vivid image of Chinese culture and having a wide influence at home and abroad.